THE roBOT BOOK WRITING METHOD

Amplify Your Authority & Acquire More Customers

Using A Book Writing Automation

With A Three Step Framework

DR. TINA FRIZZELL-JENKINS

THE roBOT BOOK WRITING METHOD

Amplify Your Authority & Acquire More Customers
Using A Book Writing Automation
With A Three Step Framework

Copyright © 2022 by Tina Frizzell-Jenkins

Library of Congress Control Number: Pending

ISBN: 978-0-9837312-9-0

Published by: Just Traders International
JTI
P.O. Box 224
Glenn Dale, MD 20720
publish@jtillc.com

Editor: Dr. Joseph Amantu & Tina Konstant
Cover Design & Illustration: Emily's World
Interior Design: jtillc.com

Printed in the USA

All rights reserved under International Copyright Law. No part of this book may be reproduced in any form except for the inclusion of brief quotations in a review, stored in a retrieval system, or transmitted in any form by any means-electronic, mechanical, photocopy, recording, or otherwise without prior express written permission of Author and or Just Traders International, LLC.

Disclaimer: This book is intended to provide accurate information in regards to the subject matter covered. All information is deemed accurate: however, it is for educational purposes only. The reader is advised to seek professional services for their unique situation.

Dedication

This work is dedicated to my wonderful great aunt Almetter Fisher-Dixon who saved my life, and to my two brothers Tony Frizzell and Till Frizzell III Whom I Love to Life.

How The roBot Book Writing Method Works for Your Business

Using The roBot Book Writing Method to write and design your book does the following:

- **Activates a Second Version of You** out in the world growing your audience.
- **Builds Belief in Your Business** without you being physically present with a potential customer.
- **Creates an Asset**... an item of ownership that is convertible to cash.

This is accomplished by designing your book **using our simple framework** that incorporates interactive tools and activities to provide your readers **with a learning experience and makes them informed buyers** in regards to the solutions your products or services offer for them.

The roBot Book Writing Method 3 Step Framework System creates an environment that can accelerate your business growth using your book as an asset by building the following:

The roBot Book Automation
The Behavioral Reaction Automation
The Business Growth Automation

Our Desire: To have **you** collaborate with our team, engage in our community and **write multiple books.**

Table of Contents

Dedication I
How The roBot Book Writing Method Works for Your Business II
Acknowledgements V
Introduction 1

THE ROBOT BOOK AUTOMATION 5

Chapter 1 7
The Business of Books 7
   Business of Books 8
      Selling Your Book Is Optional; Yet, the Cash Can Flow In. 9
      Strategic Lead Generation Tool 10
      Speaking Your Message Gets Book Sales 15
      Self-Assessment: Expert 18
Chapter 2 25
Big Bold Idea that Gets Results 25
   Big Bold Idea that Gets Results 26
      Creativity with a spark of innovation 26
      Consider the Request of the Niche Community 28
      Count the Cost… Conduct Your Market Analysis 32
Chapter 3 35
Blending Ideas: P³ Outline Formula 35
   Blending Ideas: P³ Outline Formula 36
      Picture 37
      Parable 38
      Principle 42
Chapter 4 47
Beginning Now… 47
   Beginning Now… 48
      S.T.A.R.T. 48
      Self-Assessment: Values for Business 50
      SOS 53
      Steps To Complete The Process 54
Chapter 5 69
Boost your Bottomline… Self-publish 69
   Boost Your Bottomline… Self-Publish 70
      Protect Your Intellectual Property 70
      Provide Answers Before Objections 73
      Professionally Design & Print Your roBot Book 80

THE BEHAVIORAL REACTION AUTOMATION 83

Chapter 6 85
Blazing Trails of Trust 85
   Blazing Trails of Trust 86

Self-Assessment: Trustworthiness Within Your Business Community 87
Guarantee Your Trustworthiness...90
Genuinely Love the People You Serve 91
Get Results for the Customer 91
CHAPTER 7 95
BUILD A BUZZ FOR YOUR BUSINESS 95
Build a Buzz for Your Business..96
Deliver An Experience..101
Dope Customer Reviews..102
Disseminate Vision Through Social Channels 106

BUSINESS GROWTH AUTOMATION 113

CHAPTER 8 115
BIG BUCKS BY COACHING 115
Big Bucks By Coaching 116
Create a Results-Driven Training..118
Convey Your Message In Boot Camps 120
Coach Like A Pro..123
Self-Assessment: Coaching Skills......................................127
Self-Assessment: Leadership...133
CHAPTER 9 139
BENEFITS FOR YOUR BUSINESS WITH YOUR SELF CARE 139
Benefits for Your Business with Your Self Care........................140
Maximize Your Energy with Health Hack 140
Mastery Builds the Confidence 142
Meditate To Activate Innovation..144
Self-Assessment: Creativity..148
CHAPTER 10 153
BEST BUSINESS MARKETING DECISION 153
Best Business Marketing Decision ... .154
What To Do Next..155
How To Get Help?..155
ABOUT THE AUTHOR 157
RESOURCES 159
OTHER LITERARY WORKS 161

Acknowledgements

I acknowledge my parents, Aretha & Tillman Frizzell, Jr. for being the coaches in my ear, starting from an early age, and always telling me all things are possible to them who believe, even when the world told me it was not.

I am most grateful for my family, (Willis, Tinille, & Tenise), and my extended family who continuously give me the space to serve my community and support me always.

I say thank you to all of the coaches and mentors (including my aunties) who have contributed to my personal growth. Special shout-outs to Dr. Myron Golden and Dr. Cheryl Jordan for going above and beyond the call of duty of coaching me. Lastly, to my students who entrusted me to be their coach and mentor. I learned so much from all of you. This work was possible because of God on my side and all of you. Thanks!

Introduction

This book was created to illustrate the power of a book working virtually automatically to create an influx of customers looking for your products and or services. The book acts like a Bot in that it replicates the author (you), building belief in your business before you are personally introduced to a customer. **Thus, The roBot Book Writing Method™ was born.** The book you write for your business is designed **with one overarching goal: to build the belief in your brand.** The book's message persuades and magnifies the belief that your product or service is worthy of an up-close and intimate relationship. **The roBot Book Writing Method will replicate the benefits of your business automatically through the pages of the book. This is done by adding interactive content to heighten the awareness of your brand. Interactive activities include links to assessments, surveys, posts, testimonials, templates, and personal Q&A services, to name a few.** Every time the machine (your roBot Book) resembles a human being (asking questions like an assessment) and is able to replicate certain human movements (getting someone to take actions via activity at the end of each chapter and share with another real human) and functions (video interactions) automatically the roBot Book tool is working!

There are new businesses being started every day and there are old businesses looking to scale every day and they both have one thing in common. What is that, you ask? They are all looking to get in front of new clients, to grab their attention, and to win their business.

Every business has a service or a product that gets their clients' the outcome they desire. The problem is that if no one knows that the business exists, then the outcomes that the business has to offer can't be utilized. We can all agree that we live in a world full of options. Some options are good and some not so good. Of the options available, customers can only choose from the options put before them. In many niches, there are a lot of options. Therefore, the customer has to do his/her due diligence as they make an emotional decision to make a purchase and then apply some logic to justify the purchase to themselves. That's why a book is a perfect tool to use to acquire customers.

The book can create the flare of feelings to make the purchase and provide the written justification as to why the purchase is necessary.

Yes, the purchase is necessary in order to get the results the customer wants. It is my desire that **this book will provide you with the "Cliff Notes" (i.e., abbreviated explanation) of how using a book with robotic characteristics as an asset to amplify authority and acquire more clients is the best idea and to persuade you to write your book.** There are lots of books out there with many statistics, case studies, and stories about how the process works. This book is basic and a quick read; yet, enough content to get the ball rolling or to get you to put pen to paper and create an asset for your business.

That said **if the result you desire is to become an...**

- **Authority in your niche**
- **Acquire more customers**
- **Add an Asset**

Then strap yourself in and let's get busy for the following reasons:

- Reason #1 – In the near future, hiring me and my team to help you with your book project will be the fast wat to implement the strategies in this book and help create a powerful asset you can use.
- Reason #2 – The sooner you jump-start and get results with your asset-building book project, the sooner you'll solidify your belief of what's possible.
- Reason #3 – The faster you move, the more excitement you'll build around your book project. Energy is not created or destroyed, it just converts to another form; therefore, building excitement around your book project will push your project to completion faster.

I want to help you; thus, I have structured this book to do the following:

First, make a case for using your book as a marketing and sales asset. Second, to answer questions that have dampened your excitement towards creating your book asset while stomping out limiting beliefs that hinder forward progress. Third, and lastly, to encourage you to use **The roBot Book Writing Method** to level up your business and enjoy the benefits of having clients looking for you. To do that, we will spend time focusing on adding the correct ingredients into your book so the robotic engine, so to speak, will automatically start producing the results you desire immediately.

If you want to accelerate your progress, we would love to hear from you. You can count on us to assist you with writing your book using The roBot Book Writing Method:

https://launch-help.chatwithdrtinafj.com

The roBot Book Automation

Dr. Tina Frizzell-Jenkins

Chapter 1

The Business of Books

Business of Books

"Although no one can go back and make a brand new start,
Anyone can start from now and make a brand new ending."
~ Carl Bard

My first solo book was a game-changer for me. Once I finished the book and the self-publishing process, I knew I was on to something that would add value to my current business and any business adventure in the future. I hope you picked this book up to be a game-changer for your business.

Using a book to attract the attention of intelligent and well-informed buyers, is a fabulous form of marketing and it builds authority in your niche. The root word of authority is author; therefore, it makes sense that becoming an author elevates your status in the community you are serving. In fact, becoming an author puts you in the top 1% of the population.

The first book I wrote is titled, "Real Savings Real Deductions" (currently out of print). It was a business book with fantastic tax saving strategies for entrepreneurs. The strategies helped entrepreneurs capture thousands of dollars legally. The book was so revealing that I was asked by a certain agency to stop selling the book, even though one of their own said; "this is a fine piece of work." At that time, I was a NASA engineer. I was working on the Hubble air conditioning system as a mechanical engineer. The reason I share this story is that I was not an accountant or a tax professional; yet, I was sought after to share tax-saving presentations to several referral marketing teams. The book established me as an authority in the tax field. I was an engineer who studied and learned tax strategies to keep more of the money I was earning on my full-time job and in my part-time dream-building endeavors. My family and I received great tax-savings, so I shared the information. That book was proof to me that writing a book establishes your authority, especially if the book is well done and gives the reader results. My book was well-done and certainly gave results to readers. To this day, I still glance at that book and smile.

> My name is Dr. Tina Frizzell-Jenkins, the Chief Servant and Founder of Just Traders International, LLC. My team and I AIM to help busy professionals, content creators, and entrepreneurs to write and self-publish their books in order to build authority in their niche, acquire new customers, and add asset, your book. For your FREE mini author masterclass go to chatwithdrtinafj.com.

Selling Your Book Is Optional; Yet, the Cash Can Flow In.

Along with building authority and belief with **The roBot Book Writing Method**, you will increase your influence as others begin to share and articulate the amazing results your product or services provide. You want your book to cause cash to flow in while you are flowing in increasing your influence. This is accomplished by putting a production in play and building beliefs with **The roBot Book Writing Method** as the main character. It works like this: You write a book that solves at least three problems for the community you serve. You self-publish the book and sell them and keep all the royalties. The community reads your book that incorporates **The roBot Book Writing Method** and gets results. Now, members of the community are seeking you out to help them solve their problems faster or to assist them in solving other problems.

This process allows your business to be in a position to charge $20 for your book that uses **The roBot Book Writing Method** or you can give it away for FREE. Why? The book brings a steady flow of new customers to your business's front door, be it brick and mortar or virtual. Now, you can assess the customers' requirements and provide the best service or product to them that gets them the results they desire. Plus, statistics say that a satisfied customer is very likely to buy from you again. This moves the odds more in your favor of getting a higher ticket sale or back-end sale because of **The roBot Book Writing Method**'s charm incorporated in your book and your effective manner of providing the customer with results.

Strategic Lead Generation Tool

Lead generation is a lifeline that keeps the business healthy. It is the process of identifying, attracting, and capturing the attention of potential customers. Without leads, the business could be put on life support or die. Leads come from advertisements, blogs, events, word of mouth, and yes, you guessed it, books. It can be tough to narrow down the best tool that is likely to foster the outcome you desire. The good news is that once you write the book the content is in place and ready to go, there's no need to come up with fresh content daily like it is required in a blog or post. The goal is to acquire a lead for free or for a minimum financial investment. This is definitely possible with the use of **The roBot Book Writing Method.**

A New Reality

Using **The roBot Book Writing Method** framework reduces the daily stress of constantly chasing after new leads for the business. Your goal is to get your book in the hands of many prospects daily. Once they choose to purchase, read and follow your framework, they will keep coming back to you to solve their particular problem. Your calendar and events will start to fill up effortlessly.

- Reason #1 – More readers will result in more sales, even if the marketing arm of your business is not where you want it to be, yet.
- Reason #2 – Readers are leaders and more educated consumers. Therefore, filling your pipeline with these individuals will enhance your community, amplify your authority and make space for scaling your business.
- Reason #3 – The best method to radically increase your book sales is to sell using **The roBot Book Writing Method**. I have witnessed influencers selling upwards of 50 books a day and hundreds of books a month using the robotic book concept.

A.C. knows she is supposed to write several books, but just didn't know where to start.
Too many ideas and no clear direction
Limiting beliefs about her writing skills were drowning her voice to write.
Unaware that a book could launch a business.

AC started down the path of using a quick pace RUJD (Read Up Jot Down Journal) template to accomplish her first book. After regularly attending the weekly Author Creator coaching session which is an integral part of **The roBot Book Writing Method** framework, she made a shift to tackle her own book project. Not only did she write the book, but she also launched a product business that included several spin-off products. True to her beliefs, she is back in the community, writing her next book, and has started her speaking career.

Who is this the roBot Method Book for?

Aspiring Authors	✓
Entrepreneurs	✓
Professionals	✓
Influencers	✓
Storytellers	✓
Speakers	✓
Parents	✓

This book is written for the individuals who show up in the above chart. None of you need to be elegant writers, super salespeople, or college grads. What you need most is to be driven to change your business and financial situation from your current reality to your dream reality.

The book writing can be done by the aspiring author, you, or you can choose to have a ghostwriter to deliver the project for you in your voice. When you put pen to paper or fingers to keys, you need only to follow an asset-building framework over fourteen to twenty-one days. You will gather content from a number of materials you have previously written, including training, blogs, posts, or journal notes, to name a few. Remember, the idea is to get your genius knowledge written out and put your book using **The roBot Book Writing Method** to awe future customers.

Ghostwriting does not have to be as expensive as one might think. Sometimes, the time that is saved more than makes up for the cost of the ghostwriter. The Ghostwriter gathers key information that is collected in an interview or by recordings. Within weeks or sometimes days, your voice shows up in text for your approval. For example, there is a chapter in this book that was mostly done by a ghostwriter. Can you guess which one? *Email me at guess@tinafrizzell.com and if you are correct, I will shout you out at one of my events and I will share one of my books or some other tool with you that the two of us deem relevant for your success. Feeling Lucky? You could get a 1-1 coaching conversation with me, Coach Tina FJ.* In my previous books, I never used a ghostwriter; however, to prove that the process can work, I purposely hired one to contribute to this work. My first draft of this book took less than two weeks to assemble. The ghostwriter gave me her portion in three days, and I can say that the cost was extremely reasonable, like less than $75.00 with a 20% tip (note, the more you pay the less likely you will have to spend time editing yourself to be sure your voice shows up).

Once you choose a Ghostwriter you should be prepared to articulate three key features of your product or service that you use to get results for your current clients. For instance, The roBot Book Writing Method will help the writers (or anyone up for the adventure) to create a book that is intentionally designed to 1) amp-up authority, 2) acquire customers, 3) add an asset. More about this later. For now, say it with me, "I Can Do It!" "I can write a book!"

C.H. an HR Professional – Wrote on and off for a decade but no book
Took several classes but the writing process did not connect.
Needed a book for a speaking engagement within a couple of weeks of taking the Outline Your Next Book Challenge.
Required a Book TM™ (Book Teller Machine) to collect **ALL** her royalties.

CH showed up and turned all distractions off and played full out in the Outline Your Next Book Challenge. With 5 hours of VIP coaching and 5 hours of training with Coach Tina FJ and the team, the AHA connection was formulated along with her outline. Within two weeks of taking the challenge, she used **The roBot Book Writing Method** and the book was done for her speaking engagement. Plus, she had a Book TM™ created and generated royalties before the printed copies were shipped. CH had her first book signing within a month and there was a steady flow of folks engaged and buying her book. But wait, there is more. She utilized the order bump to generate fast cash by offering a "read now" flipbook and she was able to land coaching sessions due to the upsell from her Book TM™. Get Excited!

Speaking Your Message Gets Book Sales

One of the best opportunities, if not the best opportunity, to sell books is to make the books available after a speaking engagement. Sell the books in multiples to maximize sales. Package the books in 3's or twenty or fifty. Then, provide the narrative as to why buying multiple books makes sense. Like selling them at a reduced cost and allowing the purchaser to earn a few dollars as they sell them. You can also partner with someone whose business can benefit from your book. For instance, if you are a personal trainer, you can locate a gym that is willing to pay you to advertise in the back of your book. The gym owner can now make the book available for their future gym members as an incentive to get a membership and for their current gym members as the book that adds value to their exercise routine.

The business of books is just that. It is a business. Let's do a tiny bit of math. Let's say your book sells for $20.00. You can print a short run of books; therefore, each book costs you $8.00 with some color pages. You earn a profit of $12.00. If you sold the same book through Amazon, you would be lucky to make between $3 and $5, because Amazon buys the book from you at a deep discount. To me, $12.00 is a lot better than $5.00.

Now let's just say you are a bestselling author and you are selling 40,000 books a year @ $3.00 each. With that many books, you are not likely to be mailing them out yourself. That's why we are using $3.00 per book. That adds up to $120,000. That's acceptable cash.

The average person only sells between 250 and 300 books per year if they are actively pushing sales. Selling 300 books at $12.00 per book is a whopping $3,600. Are you scratching your head and saying writing a book is a lot of work for $3,600? That doesn't cover the cost of writing and printing the book. Why bother? You get it done for the three reasons we created **The roBot Book Writing Method.**

1. Authority in your niche
2. Acquiring more customers
3. Add an Asset

These goals are fulfilled by obtaining a steady flow of customers looking for you and your services, versus you hunting the customers down. You have used your own roBot Book to make you and your business more findable by informing customers who want to do business with you.

If you are a coach and you charge $3,000 for your group coaching program and you **enroll 20 extra** students each quarter of the year as a result of them reading your book.

$3000(20)(4) = **$180,000 per year**

If you charge $10,000 for your group coaching

$10,000(20)(4) = **$800,000 per year**

Let's say you have an online course that is hands-off at this point and you sell it for $997.00. Let's say you give away 100 books so you technically lose $ 100(12) = **-$1,200**.

Let's say your roBot Book generated **30% of sales** from the folks who read the book and went online and purchased the course your book persuaded them to do.

30 ($997) = **$29,910.00 in course sales**

If you subtract what you lost from giving the books away you have still **earned…. $28,710 for course sales**. Say, "WOW!" Now, say it backward, "WOW!"

I am not aware of many businesses that could not use an extra $28,710.00, are you?

These examples are proof that by including The roBot Book Writing Method in your book project you can build authority, acquire customers, and create additional revenue in the business using your book, the asset. Somebody should be getting EXCITED!

Let's drive the point home. Imagine your book project earns you just $5000.00 in one year. In three years if you have NOT written the book your lack of action has now cost you $15,000. Those EXTRA funds could have been invested for retirement, become the down payment for an investment property, or provided medicine for a senior in your life, with money left over for you to take your dream vacation. Stop asking what if "it" doesn't work and start asking what if "it" does work. Take the expert assessment below to determine your expert status:

Self-Assessment: Expert

Below, rate yourself on a scale from 1-5 on how accurate the statements are – 1 means, "not accurate at all" and 5 means, "most accurate." The score for each answer is located within the parenthesis.

Once you've rated yourself for each statement, total up your scores and then use the Answer Key to determine your next steps.

Expert Assessment	Self-Rating
What happens when you Google your name?	
My website pops up with my social media site addresses (5)	
My trainings and a few other articles show up (3)	
I don't show up; however, folks with my name show up (0)	
What is your highest level of excitement to birth a book?	
Extremely Excited (5)	
Excited (4)	
Somewhat Excited (3)	
Not Excited (0)	
What is the status of your email list?	
I have over 5,001 names on my list (5)	
I have 1,000 - 5,000 names on my list (4)	
I have over 100 -1001 names on my list (3)	
I do not have an email list (0)	

How many years have you worked at your trade or profession?
20+ years (5)
10-19 years (4)
3-9 years (3)
0-2 years (2)
Do you own your name or desired business name?
Yes (5)
No (0)
Do you teach your content?
Yes (5)
No (0)
Do you have a website?
Yes (5)
No (0)
Do you speak to a target audience?
Yes (5)
Occasionally (3)
Nope public speaking is not my thing (0)
Have you been honored by your community, job, or social group for work that you have done well?
Yes often (5)
A few times (3)
Never (0)
Have you ever received media coverage for your work or hobby?
Yes (5)
No (0)

Denied the invitation (0)

How do you get new customers to connect with you?

Paid advertisement, challenges, podcasts, online events (5)

Lead magnets, webinars, website (3)

Nothing yet (0)

How are you connecting to potential fans through social media?

Post regularly and with videos (5)

Post inconsistently with a few videos (3)

Not posting at all (0)

How many stars would you say your customers would give rating their customer satisfaction?

Five Stars (5)

Four Stars (4)

Three Stars (3)

One Star (0)

Do you have customer events to build your brand recognition?

Yes (5)

No (0)

I have not developed a brand, yet (0)

Do you have a company logo with brand colors?

Yes (5)

Yes, I have a logo but no brand colors (3)

No (0)

Do you have a business coach?

Yes (5)

Not Currently… looking for one (3)

No, never had one (0)	
How many new leads do you get monthly?	
100+ (5)	
3-90 (4)	
1 or 30 (3)	
Do folks around you consider you knowledgeable on a specific subject?	
Very knowledgeable and they seek me out for assistance (5)	
I am thought of as the next best thing to a "professional" that normally they would have to hire (5)	
Folks do not tend to come to me for assistance (0)	
How frequent are you asked to share your knowledge on a particular subject?	
Frequently asked, in fact, they should be paying me (5)	
Sometimes I am asked to share my knowledge (3)	
Never (0)	
Can you talk about a particular topic for 3-5 minutes without notes?	
Yes, with ease and get applause (5)	
Yes, it is a struggle; however, I do get my point across (4)	
Nope, I need my notes (2)	
Total Score	

The fastest way to be seen as an expert is to write a book that helps people solve problems that matter to them. Using a technique that works is a good idea, especially when there is a track record of "it" working. In this case, it is authorship. **The roBot Book Writing Method** is a #1 tool used in building authority.

Score 0-65
Apprehensive Expert

The bad news is that your expert qualities are missing core fundamentals. This is likely not a surprise to you.

However, the good news is that you can grow and improve on your core qualities. Get some coaching to expedite the process.

Read this book with an open mind and make notes throughout. The purpose is to study, master, and apply the principles and techniques in this book. You may have to review the chapters you have already completed. Next, teach someone else to be great and gather some testimonials to share.

Score 66-78
Aspiring Expert

If your score landed you here, then you are on track to write the book that will assist you in attracting better customers. Better customers will give you better sales conversion rates.

Find a good hook for your short book, coupled with the Big Idea with Air and you will be on the right road. You will be on the road to meeting your goals, building authority, acquiring customers, and adding more revenue streams. See Chapter 4 for the Big Idea A. I. R. training,

Currently, you are likely relying on marketing strategies that are not working the best for you. No worries, **The roBot Book Writing Method** is just the framework you need to have a steady flow of the right customers.

> Score 79-100
> Authority Expert

Since your score landed you here, it is safe to say that you are the type of expert that followers love to follow. This should excite you!

Dan Kennedy said, "Certain experts, professionals, and providers do not sell their recommendations; they have the authority needed to prescribe them." Writing a book affords you the opportunity to receive instant authority at a higher level than you currently have. You get to prescribe the framework for results

Using **The roBot Book Writing Method** can give you the opportunity to prescribe the framework for results. Without a doubt, your product or service is available and just what is required. After all, they are following you and desiring to gain wisdom from you. Plus, folks are proud to be associated with an expert, especially a published expert.

> Creating an assessment is part of **The roBot Book Method**. In Chapter 4, you will find out how we create them.

Take Action Now...

Repeat the affirmation out loud and in front of an accountability partner or a mirror...

1. **I will be an author this year! It is easy! I can do it! It will work!**
2. Visualize holding the book in your hand while feeling the slickness of the cover and the weight of the book.
3. Write **The roBot Book Writing Method** outline...

Need help join:

outlineyournextbookchallenge.com

Chapter 2

Big Bold Idea that Gets Results

Big Bold Idea that Gets Results

"It's the combination: big idea with a good entrepreneur: there's nothing more powerful."

~ Bill Drayton

You are the creator of your book's Big Bold Idea. **The roBot Book writing Method** uses your Big Bold Idea as the starting point in the "roBot book" creation. This is Phase 1 of The roBot Book Writing Method Framework. Chances are your Big Idea will grow out of the first level of the Four Levels of Influence (Further explanation in Chapter 3), The Talent Reveal Level. This level of influence generally shows up when you are young. This scenario played out so well with my younger brother who is gifted musically. He plays the drums. His gift showed up between 5-10 years old.

Fast forward to later in life and the gift becomes live in a business, a book, and the related products if you are open. Another way to look at it is, **"The Big Idea" is creative and robust enough to produce profits.**

Creativity with a spark of innovation

Creativity is one thing; however, adding innovation to the equation takes the book or project to another level. When I started working on my fourth book project, I wanted to create a book that answered most of the typical questions that I receive about coaching. When you write your book using **The roBot Book Writing Method** you want to answer as many questions within the writing that you can to help the reader.

I wrote the book, "Coaching Conversations, How Anyone Can Use Proven Techniques To Breakthrough Personal and Professional Barriers" (see Resources in the rear of this book). I also wanted to create an innovative process that would allow almost anyone to be able to write a book, fast. The "Read Up Jot Down Journal" (RUJD) series was born. The idea is that you teach something in the first four chapters of the book and the last half of the book is a journal so the student/learner can document their results as they act on the information they have learned. **The roBot Book Writing Method** is the Sedan vehicle framework and the RUJD framework is the compact vehicle, so to speak.

In the coaching book, I teach about coaching in the first half of the book and tell my story. It is four chapters long. The second half of the book is a journal where my coaching clients can document coaching sessions, homework, aha moments, reflections, and get some inspiration from quotes. The process worked for me, but would it work for someone else?

A.F. is a retired senior – Desired to write a book but did not know how.
Wrote a training manual in the past for her business clients
Loves to read and listen to books…favorite thing to do
Had done some blogging

I requested my A.F. (aka my mom) who was 83 years old at the time, to use the RUJD framework and write her first book, *Community Service, Everyone Can Get Involved* (find it on Amazon). My mom has been a community service person her entire life. At the time of her writing, she was feeding the hungry, two Saturdays out of every month. She wrote the book that taught the heart of community service and told her story. In the back of the book, students get to document their community service hours and experiences in order to meet their graduation requirements. Dr. Willie Jolley was so impressed that he endorsed her book. The RUJD framework works and it can make you an author, fast.

It is also worth noting that at age 86, mom wrote her Legacy book, *Rear View Mirror Reflections: A Life Journey Of A Woman Of Color* using the beta version of **The roBot Book Writing Method**. Check it out at *AretheFrizzell.com*.

Consider the Request of the Niche Community

The "**Big Book Idea**" needs to have **A.I.R.** to establish the belief necessary for your book to work well with **The roBot Book Writing Method**. You want a Big Ideas that work effectively in the niche community you choose.

As we launch into this discussion, it is essential that you catch the vision that this book-writing exercise is not just about writing a book; it's about creating a book project that will produce profits.

From the start of the book project, there are key elements that MUST be researched, understood, and pinpointed for the best results. That's where the **A.I.R.** comes in.

Accurate Audience - **I**deal Information - **R**ight Results

Most adults are visual learners, so picture this. Think of your book being launched inside of a see-through helium-filled balloon. The higher the balloon rises; the more people can see the book and inquire about it. The exposure opens up the door for curious on-lookers to find out more about the book and the owner. This is how more books and book-related projects get sold. The right launch vehicle, in this case, **The roBot Book Writing Method** or clear helium balloon is chosen.

If you are writing a fiction or a non-fiction book, knowing the accurate audience that one will be writing to or speaking to will determine how successful your efforts will be once the Belief roBot Book is done.

ACCURATE AUDIENCE

Choosing an accurate audience has everything to do with the success of your book project. Taking some time on the front end of the project will likely result in more books sold and more products sold.

For example, non-fiction writers who are seeking to increase their authority and scale their business with their roBot Book will want to write to one of three niches at this current time. They are the Health, Wealth, and Relationship industry.

The next exercise is to narrow your niche down to a very small audience type. When you market to everybody, you market to no one. Think of the times when you go to Google to ask a question. The more specific your questions are, the better the results that Google gives you. We want to make your book and book project findable for those who are looking for what we have to offer.

I have also added to the online Training Area my Niche Narrowing Strategies document as an added bonus to save you some time when creating your Big Idea.

IDEAL INFORMATION

There are a few **DOs** and **DON'Ts** when it comes to the information you provide to the ideal audience.

DO NOT give the audience what you want them to have.

DO give the audience what the audience wants. Giving the audience what they want may require asking folks in the niche some questions or getting them to complete a survey.

DO NOT chase after an outdated topic.

DO be relevant. Trust that your audience is intelligent and on top of what is going on in their circle.

DO NOT copy the work of others word for word. It was wrong when you were in English class, and it is wrong now.

DO study, research, and trust your inner genius to provide excellent and groundbreaking or thought-provoking content.

Get Excited, Get Inspired, and Get Connected!

Excitement triggers good vibes in your mind and your body. The excitement provides the energy necessary to keep a project moving. Get inspiration because inspiration stimulates our intellect. Once the know-how juices get flowing, before you know it, you have completed another chapter of your roBot Book.

Getting connected to a writing group, and a coach will likely increase the speed of completing your Book. The accountability built into a writing group is priceless. Plus, you are more likely to hear about tools and tricks that make the writing process easier, more professional, and fun.

RIGHT RESULTS

Clarify the outcome that you want to provide to the reader or to any students of your work. It is a requirement to start with the end top of mind. What are a good majority of the readers looking to draw from your well of writing? For example, will it be humor, history, or how-to?

If you really want to wow them and get a buzz around your project, figure out the most straightforward path to getting the audience result, lay out an easy strategy, and get them to buy into the idea they have what it takes to be a winner.

Remember that a good story and a good "how-to guide" stimulate the head and gratify the heart. When the head is stimulated, it causes the body to act, which is how projects get done. When the heart is gratified, we have delicious thoughts, meditate on the process, and visualize current and future states. This reaction also pushes your roBot Book to completion.

Lastly, make sure you have correctly named your roBot Book because if the Book is not picked up, it cannot be read, and your message will not multiply, and neither will your profits

Count the Cost... Conduct Your Market Analysis

Do you want to reduce the risk of your roBot Book not being effective? Conduct market analysis. Completing a market analysis will help you to understand your customers and what is actively happening in the market your desire to do business. You want your roBot Book to be fully equipped to serve and get the results that your desired marketplace would like to have.

Another good reason to conduct a market analysis is to identify opportunities for growth that you may not have considered. One nugget unearthed could mean several additional thousands of dollars in your pocket. Perhaps what you learn could reveal a possible partnership opportunity that needs investigating or another product or service that you could extend your brand into. The possibilities are endless, so be open.

If you don't have the budget for a full-out analysis, then get creative. Ask for input or suggestions in chat groups, create an online poll, or my favorite, use your phone. Your phone has a private audience that has opinions. They will tell you if the title of your book works or that it needs work. Be careful to poll folks on your phone who are worth providing the information you can take seriously.

Let's Review:

	The "**Big Book Idea**" has to have a lot of **A.I.R.**	
A	**A**ccurate Audience	
I	**I**deal Information	
R	**R**ight Results	

Take Action

1. Dedicate a minimum of three hours of "think" time over a five-day period and do a brainstorming exercise to determine the AIR of your Big Idea and document the results.
2. Put an accountability partner in place to help you follow through on your schedule.
3. Poll a small audience in your niche for Big Idea feedback.

Chapter 3

Blending Ideas: P³ Outline Formula

Blending Ideas: P³ Outline Formula

"There is no greater agony than bearing an untold story inside you" ~ Maya Angelou

The blending of ideas into a rhythmic flow of words using **The roBot Book Writing Method** is the way to build and outline a book that will whisper to the reader, read me, read me, read me, please, read me. The words almost force a smooth melody to accompany the words in your head or a dramatic beat to simulate the blood flow. The words are designed to cause a reaction. The first reaction is to tell me more and a close second reaction would be to pull out the credit card. All of this creativity comes from the Creator and the gifts and talents that you are born with, which you use to influence those you are called to serve through the ministry of business.

You can effectively share what you have to offer your customers using the P³ Structure. This structure guides the customer through visualization in a picture, an analogy in a parable, and the understanding of the offer through the principles. Below is how the P³ works with Coach Tina's roBot Book; however, when you put into play your roBot Book you will use the system to tell your customer your story. For example, if you review the table of contents for this book (which is the book outline), you will see patterns of lettering that tend to be attractive to the eye. This gives the outline a flow. Notice how I was intentional about using the letter "B" in Chapter Titles and the subtitles start with the same letter. Titles or Subtitles can all start with nouns or verbs or the words can rhyme. The idea is to create something that looks good,

```
THE BUSINESS OF BOOKS............................................................
    BUSINESS OF BOOKS ........................................................
        Selling Your Book Is Optional; Yet, the Cash Flows In. ............
        Strategic Lead Generation Tool..........................................
        Speaking Your Message Gets Book Sales...........................
CHAPTER 2..................................................................................
BIG BOLD IDEA THAT GETS RESULTS........................................
    BIG BOLD IDEA THAT GETS RESULTS ................................
        Creativity with a spark of innovation.................................
        Consider the Request of the Niche Community...................
        Count the Cost... Conduct Your Market Analysis .............
CHAPTER 3..................................................................................
BLENDING IDEAS: P³ OUTLINE FORMULA......................................
    BLENDING IDEAS: P³ OUTLINE FORMULA ............................
        Picture ........................................................................
        Parable........................................................................
        Principle......................................................................
```

sounds good, and conveys the right information. Create your roBot Book outline with rhythm. The book, <u>Words that Sell</u> by Richard Bayan is a good thesaurus-like tool to assist with finding words. The Following is the P³ Structure:

P³ Structure = Picture + Parable + Principle

Picture

Pictures are the eyes when needed at a later date to retell the story, remind us of the mystery and warm the soul with good memories. When I think of God and the Creation, I think wow. Wow, because I was made in His image; therefore, I was made to be creative. You were made to be creative. God did not appear to be in a rush over those seven days of creation. Maybe because He was demonstrating patterns and principles that He didn't want us to miss. For example, He complimented Himself at the completion of each day. He said, "that was good." Perhaps we should take a page out of God's playbook and take time to say the work we have done is good. Also, remember to compliment others when their work is good. Giving that level of energy can only produce fruit that is good and contagious.

Parable

A parable is used to illustrate a spiritual or moral lesson. Jesus used this form of communication when He wanted to get folks thinking beyond their same old same old thinking patterns. The same communication style can be used since business owners, professionals, and entrepreneurs endeavor to have meaningful conversations with the community they serve. The genesis of their expert conversations can stem back to birth. It is my belief that we are born with influence and some manifest that influence early in life while others seem to stumble upon it later in life. Before we take a look at the third P. I want to pause to share the **4 Level of Influence Model** because it may help you to get in tune with your gifts/expertise. Remember, your Big Idea for your roBot Book is usually tied to your expertise.

I created the **4 Level of Influence Model** to demonstrate how our personal gifts can show up in life. The four levels are the Talent

Reveal stage, the Talent Cultivation stage, the Talent Magnification stage, and the Talent Touch stage.

Talent Reveal Stage

In the Talent Reveal stage, a child's gift has a way of showing up and likely surprising the child that something is different; however, pleasantly nice. The child **_Self Observes_** the gift. Perhaps the child realizes that he or she can play the piano without knowing how to read music, calculate math equations quickly in their head, or they can fix stuff naturally without instruction. Soon after the realization sinks in, they figure out the **_Self Potential_**. If I sing for the grown-ups, I get a treat. That's when the **_Show off_** opportunities come into play. I child finds a way to _Show off_ for the company to get recognition. The child already is using the gift to influence a result, even if that result is to get a treat.

Talent Cultivation Stage

In this stage of developing influence, one realizes that if they **_Practise_**, the gift can be improved or made better; therefore, dedicated time is allotted to work towards perfecting the gift. Next, one must **_Prepare;_** and that not only includes. It also includes studying books and others who have already shown themselves as experts. Next comes the talent show or performing at the **_Playhouse._** The individual is ready to display the gift in a more public setting. Influence grows out of the preparation. Perhaps this is the first time someone is offered a significant amount of money to showcase his or her skills. This is building their influence in their niche.

Talent Reveal Stage

At this skill level, there are opportunities to build expert status, and one must build **Confidence**. This can come by the rinse and repeat method of doing something over and over again. By repeating a skill and improving that skill not only is **Confidence** built, but **Competence** can be seen from others looking on from the outside. By staying true to one's self, and with continuous gift growth, **Credibility** cultivates.

Talent Touch Stage

At this level of influence, an individual has grown past personal growth into the realm of assisting others to improve. The mission becomes **Cultivating** the **Brilliance** of others. He or she uses **Consulting** and **Coaching** to add positive contributions and to assist in changing lives for the better.

This is where **The roBot Book Writing Method** gets to show up and shine on behalf of you and your business. The book product is created with links, assessment tools, videos, and other learning materials to give your reader an experience along with ushering them to a predetermined result and physiologically further connecting them to the author, you. This is exactly what you want your roBot Book to do, just as I am trusting that you are getting to know me better through this work. Now for the third P.

Principle

Principles are bound by the law of nature and will not change. When using **The roBot Book Writing Method**, remember how essential it is to keep the excitement high while designing and building it because energy is neither created nor destroyed it converts to a different form. You want a high energy input in your design and you want a high energy output in the sales of your roBot Book.

Walter P. Chrysler tells the story, "I know a man that is a genius in the insurance industry; yet, he could not make a living selling it. I also know Stanley Gettis who knew 1/10 of the insurance knowledge yet after 20 years, he retired because he made a fortune selling insurance. His success was not 'knowledge' it was enthusiasm. One of the secrets of success is enthusiasm. **Get Excited!**

Let's review with an example-

We use a strategy called P^3. When an exponential is used in math you are saying you want something increasing quickly. When writing your non-fiction book especially, you want your reader to be able to move through your written material quickly to get the understanding so they can implement the results.

EXAMPLE roBOT BOOK OUTLINE

I. Introduction

Tell the reader how to read your roBot Book for best results and why the roBot Book exists. Explain the outcomes of the roBot Book. Give a brief summary of what they can expect from the roBot Book and the number one possible result. Add a call to action link (calendar or guided webpage/funnel).

II. Major Concept (Create this step for all chapters)

    A. **Primary concept** (Paint a Word Picture)

        1. Help Content

        2. Help Content

    B. **Secondary concept** (Tell a Parable)

        1. Help Content

        2. Help Content

    C. **Third concept** (Teach a Principle)

        1. Help Content

        2. Help Content

            a. More help

            b. More help

III. Conclusion

Give a summary of how your product and services benefit your customer. Remind them of some of the key points you have explained in your roBot Book. Tell them the three next steps required to move their needle closer to getting their solution with your product or service. Let them know you are available to help and give them your contact information.

Powerful Key SIMPLE Secrets to a Successful Outline

To achieve an effective outline, these 3 things must occur...

- *Simple Tip #1*

    Get the Outline done using the **P³** Formula.

- *Simple Tip #2*

    Get a rhythm and rhyme flowing through the sub-category titles.

- *Simple Tip #3*

    Get the reader's attention with a guided tour of the content on the Table of Contents

If you would like some help with your book writing journey that is designed to keep your calendar full:

https://launch-help.chatwithdrtinafj.com

Take Action

1. Write your story so that that your ideal audience can identify with it.
2. Do a visual exercise where you take an object and describe it in so much detail someone else can see it with their eyes closed. Make sure to incorporate all 5 senses.
3. Identify two other stories that you can share with your ideal audience and tie a business growth or a life principle to it.

Dr. Tina Frizzell-Jenkins

Chapter 4

Beginning Now...

Beginning Now...

> *"Every day is a chance to begin again. Don't focus on the failures of yesterday, start today with positive thoughts and expectations."* ~ Catherine Pulsifer

The "getting started" with a lot of projects, causes some folks to quit before they start, because of the age-old question, "where do I begin?" **The roBot Book Writing Method** is easy to jump-start, so I am going to give you the beginning process and some tools to move forward.

S.T.A.R.T.

S.T.A.R.T. is the acrostic for you guessed it Start. Let's get going!

> *Schedule*: Create a weekly schedule that agrees with your schedule. This may require that you make some sacrifices to get the project done. If you write 600 words, twice a day, or 1200 words, once a day, in 10 days, you will have written 12,000 words. 12,000 words equate to about 50 pages of text.

> *Test the Big Idea:* Testing your Big Idea is essential when it comes to writing the book that the community you serve is ready for and will read to get the desires they want. Go back and review the A.I.R. concept in Chapter 4 and then begin the process. You can do it!

Accountability: This is key. Successful folks have accountability partners or coaches in their corner. This is a clue. Oprah has a coach, Tony Robbins has a coach, Coach Tina FJ has two coaches. Be accountable to someone. Once, one of my fellow mastermind colleagues challenged us to make a wager to keep a goal on track. One guy agreed to pay his x-wife $10,000 if he did not meet his goal. He said, "I am not paying her, I will hit the goal." I am not saying you have to do something that drastic; but, don't make it easy or you might as well not bother to make it a challenge.

Resources and Tools: In order to get a job or project done the quickest and with the best result, using the correct tools are essential. The following is a good starter list of resources to make the book writing/book building business a better experience:

1. The roBot Book Method
2. Word or a writing software
3. Grammarly or an editing software
4. Word Hippo – an online word resource
5. Paymetosocialize.com – GetResponse autoresponder or similar tool used to communicate with your customers
6. Click Funnels – Funnel software is used to create your Book TM so you can collect your royalties.
7. Assessment Software – TypeForm.com
8. Stripe - An online gateway to accept payments

As you are have making forward progress in your understanding of creating a roBot book as an asset let's pause to determine if your heart is really into launching your book business from the start or on a higher level. What you value has a lot to do with what you do or don't do; therefore, take this Business Values Assessment to determine how much you value entrepreneurship/business.

Self-Assessment: Values for Business

Below, rate yourself on a scale from 1-5 on how accurate the statements are – 1 means, "not accurate at all" and 5 means, "most accurate." The score for each answer is located within the parenthesis.

Once you've rated yourself for each statement, total up your scores and then use the Answer Key to determine your next steps.

Values Assessment for Business	Self-Rating
I get excited to sell my products /services.	
I am serious about leaving a financial legacy	
For me, time is more valuable than money.	
I am a self-starter.	
Networking is a necessary task for my business growth.	
I am a continuous learner.	
I value coaching and I have a coach.	
I am curious to learn more about my industry	
I am on the lookout for meaningful relationship and stakeholders that align with my mission.	

I am honing my negotiation skills.	
I am aware of basic business tax responsibilities and I have a tax representative.	
I have a business strategy.	
I am a strategic and creative thinker.	
I have business goals.	
I revisit my business mission regularly.	
I am considered an authority in my niche.	
I desire to serve my clients at the highest levels.	
I am continuously looking for creative ways to give my clients an experience along with the results they desire.	
I am open to responsible family members and friends working alongside of me in my business endeavours.	
Total Score	

You tend to be true to your values. In fact, you will not consistently perform a task or stay on a mission that you do not value without making yourself miserable or ill. The Business Value's Assessment can be used as a looking glass into your persona to see if business ownership is truly a desire of yours.

Score 0-64
You Don't Value Entrepreneurship/Business

The bad news is **your drive to be a business owner appears to be missing**; therefore, your lack of consistency will likely show-up.

No worries, lots of folks have not considered becoming an author as the start of business ownership if done correctly.

Do you desire to earn income like presented in Chapter #1 of **The roBot Book Writing Method?** If yes, this method can definitely get you started and to the finish line.

Read **The roBot Book Writing Method** with an open mind and perhaps you may have a value shift once you reframe thoughts concerning authorship, entrepreneurship and business. Retake the assessment after you do the reading and activities.

> Score 65-84
> Yes! You Value Entrepreneurship/Business

It is not one of your highest values; so, understand at times you may have other competing values. Those values may slow you down from getting the results you desire quickly.

Writing and publishing a book will increase your authority instantly when the book is release, and the content helps folks. Folks will AUTOMATICALLY start to share the good news for them that your book has created.

The roBot Book Writing Method is famous for creating automation with a book. Your roBot Book can position your business to create another stream of income, because your book is an asset that is convertible to cash.

outlineyournextbookchallenge.com

> Score 85-100
> Yes! You Highly Value Entrepreneurship/Business!

Since your score landed you here, you definitely value entrepreneurship/business. You likely have a business or are seriously thinking of starting a business.

Dan Kennedy said, "If you want to be liberated from selling, if you want the authority to prescribe, I always advise writing and publishing at least one book."

Coach Tina FJ says, "If you want to be liberated from selling, if you want the authority to prescribe, I always advise writing and publishing at least one book that is specifically designed with automation to acquire customers effortlessly."

Using **The roBot Book Writing Method** can be very valuable to your existing business or to a business you are launching. If you should like support contact us at connect@coachtinafj.com

SOS

When we start a "Do It Yourself" project, it is generally good to have an expert on standby to seek advice from or to call on when we get in a little over our heads. This is a good idea and process to follow when writing a book, too. When I did my first solo project, it was a "Do It Yourself" project where I subcontracted out everything but the writing. I also had to create a process that worked with my way of learning and interacting with the world skills like everything else I had to learn to do in life. I was a project & program manager for NASA, so I had those skills. Wisdom also told me to tap into the knowledge of a couple of individuals that were immersed in book writing so I could get GOOD counsel. I was determined not to have my book like "I" did it or worse be like folks I have come into contact with that their book… the one that they were holding in their hand was so poorly done that it was an embarrassment to them.

It is okay to get help. In fact, I believe it is the best idea. Join **The roBot Book Writing Method** family and let us help you make authorship a reality for the first time or anytime thereafter.

outlineyournextbookchallenge.com

Steps To Complete The Process

Use the following as a quick guide:

CREATE TITLE & SUB-TITLE, OUTLINE BOOK, CONNECT WITH EDITOR AND COVER DESIGNER. LAST-MINUTE RESEARCH ON THE TOPIC.
WRITE YOUR ORIGIN STORY (for use in the book). CONTRACT WITH COVER DESIGNER & GET THE FRONT COVER DONE.
WRITE ACKNOWLEDGEMENTS, DEDICATIONS, NOTES FROM THE AUTHOR/INTRODUCTION.

WRITE CHAPTERS 1-3.
SOLICIT INFLUENCER TO WRITE FOREWORD.

WRITE CHAPTERS 4-7.

WRITE CHAPTERS 8-10.

CREATE JOURNAL PORTION (if appropriate).
REVIEW WORK WITHIN GRAMMARLY.
CONTRACT WITH EDITOR.
COPYRIGHT.
GET A BAR CODE.
THE EDITING PROCESS STARTS.
CONTRACT WITH INTERIOR DESIGNER.
FINAL COVER DESIGN DONE.

START INTERIOR DESIGNER ALIGNING MANUSCRIPT AND GET PRINT-READY.

MANUSCRIPT IN PDF READY FOR PUBLISHING.

We have covered in detail the Big Idea and how to create your Outline in earlier chapters. Next, we will take a closer look at how to create your roBot Book.

Content - The roBot Book Writing Method recommends a minimum of a ten-chapter book if your goal is to give your customer an in-depth look into your products or services. We recommend a book around 80 pages if your goal is to highlight a specific product or service.

<u>Content Example for a Podiatry Practice:</u>

Dr. Tina Frizzell-Jenkins

Copyright Page

Dedication Page

Table of Contents

Acknowledgment Page

Foreword

Introduction/Book Intent

Chapter 1- What is Podiatry and the #1 solution you get for your clients? Share what makes your Podiatry practice stand out from the others in your community. Add highlights from your origin story to introduce yourself to the reader.

Assessment

Activity

Chapter 2 – Who can best benefit from a Podiatrist? Teach the reader something about Podiatry that they might not know. Show off your expertise.

Activity

Chapter 3 – What are the common objections to NOT getting services from a Podiatrist? Share what can be expected if someone that needs a Podiatrist does not get the care they need.

Chapter 4 – Share the typical Podiatry services and the outcomes. Explain what is unusually involved in a Podiatry assessment and why.

Assessment

Activity

Chapter 5 –Share your Podiatry specialty #1 and your solution.

Activity

Chapter 6 – Share your Podiatry specialty #2 and your solution.

Activity

Chapter 7 - Share your Podiatry specialty #3 and your solution.

Assessment

Activity

Chapter 8 – Provide Podiatry Case Studies

Activity

Chapter 9 – Provide 3-7 tips on preventive health care from a Podiatry perspective.

Activity

Chapter 10 –Conclusion with a more in-depth biography to demonstrate your expertise

Activity

NOTE: *Make sure all chapters start on a page with an odd number.*

Assessment – Use assessments throughout your book to get the reader to self-identify where they are so they can be clear if the timing is NOW to use your products or services.

Activities – Provide the reader with activities that cause them to start taking "mini" actions. Their small steps will bring them clarity to determine if attempting to get to the solution alone works for them or if they could use some assistance. **Using The roBot Book Writing Method** we put our activities at the end of each chapter. This also provides another opportunity to reinforce what they read in the chapter.

Calendar – Use an online calendar software like

https://calendly.com or https://www.oncehub.com

that will allow customers to book time on your calendar when you determine it is best to meet with new customers.

Funnels – I like to call Funnels (Click Funnels)the one-stop website. Using a funnel to host your roBot Book page is what we recommend. Depending on how you want to connect with your customer you may need another funnel to host the following:

- A product page to let your customers know what you have to offer
- A challenge page/ event page to steer your customer in the direction of a learning event

Editor - There are three basic types of editing and lastly, a proofreader checks the formatting, typographical error, and, any missed mistakes before printing.

- Content editor – review the plot, characters, writing craftmanship
- Line Editor – reviews & discusses the style & flow
- Copy Editor – corrects grammar, spelling, punctuation, and small inconsistencies

To save some time and money I generally do the following before I give my manuscript to the editor:

- Use Word spell check function
- I use Grammarly
- I have a couple of trusted individuals to review the project
- I use Text to Audio to listen to the roBot Book
- I get the book formatted in WORD by a freelancer on Fiverr

Write your origin story. This is the story about your business journey that allows you to connect with your ideal customer. Make sure you are strategic and highlight the point in your story that shows you were where your customer is now and where they can dream to be. Weave in 2 or 3 principles that provide wisdom for your customers. Also, tell them about how you became the expert.

Get your **Cover design** done by a freelancer on Fiverr, or similar comapny. You can use a pre-designed cover from reedsy.com.

Acknowledgments – Keep it short, be since, give specifics, and thank everyone that helped to make your book project a reality.

Dedication – Usually the person(s) named has been impactful to you.

Book Intent /Introduction – Shares how the book came about, why the book was written, the outcomes that can be expected and it has a bit of mystery to get the reader interested in reading more.

Foreword – If possibly get an influencer in the community you are writing to and ask them to speak to a specific point or two in your book that has worked for them.

Copyright your book - http://copyright.gov

Barcode – We use http://myidentifiers.com. They can be purchased one at a time or in bulk. Remember each product needs its own barcode. For example, if you have an eBook, a paperback book, and a hardcover book with the same name and information they all need their own separate barcode.

Interior Book Designer – The person formats your manuscript, adds design, and gets it print-ready.

Printing Your Book - You can use a local printer or Amazon to print your book. The key is to make sure the size of the book and the layout are properly done so that your print job looks professional. ALWAYS get a proof copy before you request a large print job.

Schedule on your calendar dedicated times to write. Create mini win goals like the completion of two chapters. Give yourself deadlines that have consequences, if they are not met. The more substantial the consequences the more likely you will hit your goal dates on schedule or ahead of schedule.

PRESELL YOUR BOOK

Use Instagram, LinkedIn, other social media platforms and your phone contact list to ask for book pre-sells. This is a numbers game. You want to make a lot of offers for folks to buy and you will get sales.

The first requirement is to create a stripe account and link it to a simple Buy Now funnel. This is not a SALES funnel. The Sales funnel will be created later. You will be sending the buyers to your simple "Buy Now" funnel. You will need a domain for your funnel. I suggest creating a sub-domain from your book domain.

For example., presell.Book_Name.com

Second, create a "Thank-you" page flyer for your book with the book cover and add names of pre-sell customers and use it on your social platforms. Folks like doing what others are doing. Wait to get about 15 names before you start posting or sharing the flyer (see below).

Let's get started…

Follow the script below for presell of your book **via a POST**. **DO NOT DEVIATE**

Author: I am excited to announce I have a book coming out. Who wants to be in it for free? Inbox me.

Response: When any positive responses show up in your inbox take the next action

Author: I am pre-selling my book and for the first 20-50 to pre-order, I will mention them in my book.

Response: How much is it?

Author: Great, it is $20 + $4.97 S&H and it would be awesome if you could purchase today. I have a short window to get the names to my book designer. Do you want the link?

Response: Yes

Author Response: Done

Author: Thanks again, stay tuned for book launch excitement.

After you have several (20-50) prepaid books add the names to the flyer and post to add excitement.

Follow the script below for the presell to an **INDIVIDUAL via INBOX. DO NOT DEVIATE**

Author: I am excited to announce I have a book coming out. I would love to be able to mention you in the book for FREE.

Response: Thanks for thinking of me.

Author: I am pre-selling my book, "Your Book Name" and for the first 20-50 to pre-order, I will mention them in my book.

Example: I am pre-selling my book "TITLE" and for the first 20-50 that pre-order, they will get a "shout out" in the book. Be part of history as the **Library of Congress*** has accepted my book. The book will live on there forever.

*If your book has not been accepted by the Library of Congress you cannot use this. They can still get the shout-out of their names in the back of the book. To get your book in the Library of Congress you must apply on their website. You can also get creative and give away something else that grabs your potential customer's attention.

Response: How much is it?

Author: Great it is $20 + $4.97 S&H and it would be awesome if you could purchase today. I have a short window to get the names to my book designer. Do you want the link?

Response: Yes

Author: Send the Buy Now Link

Response: Done

Author: Thanks again, stay tuned for book launch excitement.

After you have several (20-50) prepaid books add the names to the flyer and post to add excitement.

Script for the phone: DO NOT DEVIATE

Please consider preordering our book, "The Book Title." For the first 20-30 folks that pre-order, we will give a "shout out" in the book. Be part of history as the Library of Congress has accepted our book. The book will live on there forever. (or- Be a part of history. Books live on forever, see your name in print)

https://...

The reason for going through all the steps is to get folks involved with you and talking about and thinking about your book project. The more involved the more likely they are to purchase. There are exceptions to the rule. Some folks will just buy. ☺

You have likely heard that the money is in the follow-up. This works for all scenarios where someone has said yes or maybe.

I am circling back to all that originally said "yes" to the book. I don't want anyone to miss out on being in the book because life happened. Lastly, be part of history as the Library of Congress has accepted our book. The book will live on there forever with your name in it! (Change this statement if your book has not been accepted by the Library of Congress to Books live on forever and you get to see your name in print. That's exciting!)

https://...**Create a Post**

I am shouting out friends and family that are supporting

Add a link: https://...

Name of Book

Book Subtitle

The following is the social flyer we decided to post:

Dr. Tina Frizzell-Jenkins

EXAMPLE FLYER:

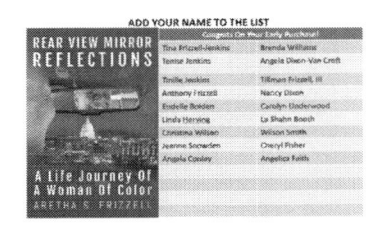

The following is the page that actually went in the back of this book:

We are here to help if you so desire:

https://launch-help.chatwithdrtinafj.com

Take Action

1. S.T.A.R.T.
2. SOS… Put someone on stand-by / Hire help.
3. Steps to finish… write the vision and make it plain.

Dr. Tina Frizzell-Jenkins

Chapter 5

Boost your Bottomline… Self-publish

Boost Your Bottomline... Self-Publish

*"You can always edit a bad page.
You can't edit a blank page."* ~ Jodi Picoult

One great thing about **The roBot Book Writing Method** is that it is created to "Book Your Business" solid. Once you get your manuscript ready for print, it is time to publish your work and let your content and solutions, camouflaged as a roBot book, go to work for you. However, first, the manuscript has to be published. One method of publishing is self-publishing and that is my preference. Self-publishing is a series of actions that are taken to get the book from a manuscript to a physical book you can hold in your hand or sell electronically. Let's review a couple of the key areas that need one's attention to complete the process.

Protect Your Intellectual Property

Protecting your intellectual property is key when it comes to keeping your genius supplying money to you, versus the thief prowling about, waiting to see whom he may devour for his own benefit. Your intellectual property is your hidden treasure. Think about an old movie when a team of folks went out in search of a hidden treasure using a map. A real-life story of a hidden treasure of gold coins and gems said to be worth more than $2 million was found in the Rocky Mountains. The spoils were located in an ornate, Romanesque box weighing 40 pounds and approximately 10x10 inches. It took over ten years for the treasure to be found. The clues were provided on a map and within a poem. Fenn's hidden treasure became a thing and it attracted tens of thousands of people on the hunt. Unfortunately, four folks lost their lives looking. Fenn's first set of clues showed up in his **self-published** book, "The Thrill of the Chase." Finn released a few more clues after the last fortune hunter's death (it still took several more years for the treasure to be found) because he said that the hunt was meant to be fun. Fin said, he never meant for anyone to lose their life. Something else stood out to me that Finn said. He said to remember, "I was eighty years old when I hid my chest." That said to me that the likelihood of the chest being in a highly dangerous place out over a cliff is very low. Sometimes, in the quest to do something new, we make up in our minds that it has to be risky and unbearably difficult. Much like self-publishing to some; however, it is not. It is a process that, when systematically done correctly, produces a book worthy to be sold by the author.

Intellectual property is such a big deal that the federal and state governments had to get involved to keep order and ensure lawful conduct. The Government has a patent, trademark, and copyright laws (more in-depth training on YouTube: IP@tinafrizzell.com). Since we are writing books, we will concern ourselves with copyrighting.

A Copyright is the exclusive right of the author or creator of a literary or artistic property (such as a book, movie, or musical composition) to print, copy, sell, license, distribute, transform to another medium, translate, record, or perform or otherwise use (or not use) and to give it to another by will. As soon as a work is created and is in a tangible form (such as writing or taping) the work automatically has federal copyright protection. On any distributed and/or published work, a notice should be affixed stating the word copyright, copy, or ©, with the name of the creator and the date of copyright (which is the year of first publication). The notice should be on the title page or the page immediately following and for graphic arts in a clearly visible or accessible place.

Copyrights cover the following: literary, musical, and dramatic works, periodicals, maps, works of art (including models), art reproductions, sculptural works, technical drawings, photographs, prints (including labels), movies, and other audiovisual works, computer programs, compilations of works and derivative works, and architectural drawings. Items not subject to copyright are short phrases, titles, extemporaneous speeches or live unrecorded performances, common information, government publications, mere ideas, and seditious, obscene, libelous, and fraudulent work. For any work created from 1978 to date, the copyright is good for the author's life, plus 50 years, with a few exceptions such as work "for hire" which is owned by the one commissioning the work, for a period of 75 years from publication. After that, it falls into the public domain. Many, but not all, countries recognize international copyrights under the Universal Copyright Convention, to which the United States is a party.

Go to copyright.gov to complete the legal documentation. Upon completing that process, you have legally made your book your intellectual property. Be careful to use the ".gov" site as opposed to a third-party site.

> Notice how I wrote this last section using the P³ Structure from **The roBot Book Writing Method**. I started creating a **picture** of a manuscript that would be used in self-publishing. Then I told a **parable/story** about someone that had successfully self-published. Lastly, I taught the **principle** of how to protect your work and that is copywriting.

Provide Answers Before Objections

One sure way to increase the bottom line is to eliminate the anxieties of potential customers so they can feel at ease and at peace as they decide to do business with you. In Chapter 6, we will discuss how Behavioral Reaction Automation works as you build trust with readers' soon-to-be customers. Nonetheless, you have to start building trust with your roBot Book and this can be accomplished by providing the expert help readers need to get over their biggest hurdles. Working within the framework of **The roBot Book Writing Method** can make the big hurdle look like tiny steps that you only need some assistance to jump over. Perhaps, you are able to write the book or at least start the book writing process alone. In fact, it is our desire that the reader is able to launch their book project from the information we share.

HURDLES

Even if I write the book, I am not a salesman, so the books will end up stacked up in my garage.

Writing a book using typical or outdated approaches may result in books stacking up in the garage; however, using a framework like **The roBot Book Writing Method** creates buying energy around your book. That energy has buyers not only looking for you but asking for more of you and what you have to offer. Would it be okay if customers are looking for you and booking your calendar? Say, "YES!"

I have nothing new or original to say and I am nobody famous. Why should someone want to read my book?

Most people are not famous and they are likely to relate to you and your story more than they would the superstar on the television. The first hurdle they have to get over with the superstar is what is real and what is for the rating. Regular people need inspiration from other regular people. People want to be able to imagine themselves in real-life scenarios, not make-believe. You are an original and you are perfectly and wonderfully made to be the unique you. The way you frame your story, (even if something similar has happened to someone else) your story is original to you. There are folks out there that can only receive the message you have to offer. Truly they can only receive it if it comes from you.

I get overwhelmed at the thought of starting the book so I don't

It is perfectly understandable that one might get overwhelmed when starting to write a book as the framework for getting it done seems to be locked away in a vault for those that are not connected to a fancy publishing company. Fortunately for those that want the vault combination, I have figured it out and I have opened the vault numerous times to write several books and help many others write books, too. Plus, I included the three-step framework for **The roBot Book Writing Method** in this book and a step by step process so you can write your book, too. In chapter 2, you identify your Big Idea and that gets the dominos out of the box. Completing the outline in chapter 3 starts the book writing dominos to fall down and then there is no stopping the forward momentum.

HURDLES

Writing a book is hard and it costs too much to get help.

When you first learned to tie your shoes, it was hard. When you first learned to add and spell everyday words, it was hard. When you first learned to drive, it was hard. I am sure you could think of other examples that before you learned how to do them, they were hard, too. However, once you learned them, they added so much value to your life that you likely would be crippled to some extent without them. Writing a book is only hard until you know how to do it. Just like someone helped you learn other life skills, my team and I are available to equip you to write a book, fast. Many times, not knowing how to do something can cost you more money than knowing how to do that thing. Take driving, for example. How much would it cost you yearly if you had to pay a chauffeur to take you everywhere, versus jumping in your car and driving yourself? Your book, hidden inside of you, is costing you more, lying dormant, than demonstrating value to those who could use it and not dropping dollars on your doorstep. Are you to stop stepping over the cash and start catching the cash? Say, "I'm Ready!"

I am not a good writer.

Thankfully, being a good writer is not an absolute requirement because of technology and freelancers that are incredible. It is more important that you have an enormous desire to share your story, your expertise, the roadmap to creating success for those that you are called to serve. The roBot Book Writing Method is a tool that will help you through the writing process. I'm dyslexic and was told I would not make it through Engineering school, yet I did. I can teach you if you are coachable.

I do not have enough material.

It may be true that your materials are limited; however, there are some short books out there that are powerful. Every book does not have to be hundreds of pages. In fact, one of my favorite books is only about 38 pages long. Can you remember a time when you sat down and finished a quick read that you enjoyed and added a lot of value to your life? Quick reads are enjoyable and you also feel so accomplished when you are finished. Experts, professionals, and content creators often say that they do not have enough material. Generally, through some coaching conversations, we are able to uncover enough writing materials to create a book or two. We are here to help you think outside of the box to create the book project that works for you.

HURDLES

Too Busy, I just don't have the time.

Typically, when it comes to increasing authority, assets, or alliances, wealthy people don't say they don't have time. They schedule a time to add value to their life and their financial portfolio. Folks who are hungry for change and desire a different outcome than what they are currently experiencing, pause, peek at the practices of the affluent, and play to win. Are you hungry? Say, "I'm Hungry!"

The whole process is too long and complicated.

The roBot Book Writing Method is proof that writing your book does not have to take long and be complicated. Following a focused schedule and taking one step at a time is the key to getting through all of the simple steps. Typically, it is not the steps that cause you to get hung up and stuck. It is your limiting beliefs that need to be destroyed. That's where the community can really help. Writing your book alongside other writers in a group coaching program or masterminds can really be value-added to your book writing journey.

I can never get published

Self-publishing is in and the best part is you get to keep all of the royalties. You are creating an asset and an asset is an item that is convertible to cash. In chapter 5, all of the steps are shown with an explanation. You can do it yourself or allow us to assist you, either way, you get to keep all of the royalties.

HURDLES

"I tried this book writing and publishing journey and I did not have success. What is it about, The roBot Book Writing Method that is different from the other investments I have made in book programs, and I still don't have a book?"

Let's discuss it. All work works. The fact that you invested in yourself is commendable. You grew from those experiences. You now know what to look for that is likely not going to get you the result you desire. You know whose voice you are unable to hear well enough to move the needle in your business and life. Lastly, you have gained the wisdom to discern what is likely the next best step for you. Trust yourself. You are armed and ready for what is next for you. Without risk, there are no rewards. Don't look back and turn into a pillar of salt on your way to safety.

How is The roBot Book Writing Method Different?

The roBot Book Writing Method is different because it has you specifically in mind. The method is starting with you now in the moments when you are reading this book and interacting with this book. The book is equipping you with the knowledge you need to assess if the expert creating tool is working for you now and will continue to work for you after you finish this book.

How much have you grown through this book and how much have you learned about yourself? How willing are you to stretch yourself outside of your comfort zone to allow your expertise to flourish and flow beyond the boundaries of your stopgaps into the hemisphere of your dreams? **The roBot Book Writing Method** is working on you now and it will work on your potential customers when you launch your Book. It will be your belief-building tool that will keep your calendar booked with prospects you get to choose to be clients.

I don't make financial decisions without my spouse or significant other.

Books have been printed since around 1489. For many years they have been proven to be the #1 sales asset for building authority, trust, and filling the calendar with potential customers and clients. The more people that read your book the more money you will make. Lastly, one of the best ways to create your book asset is to use **The roBot Book Writing Method** that is found in this book.

Hurdles were designed in the track and field arena to be jumped over as the runner makes his or her way to the finish line. Life is our field and the hurdles show up. We need only to jump over them, get up when we fall, run some more until we cross the finish line to collect the asset available to us. There are some assets, like a high school diploma, that no one can take from us. You earned it and you leverage it to take you to and through the next sets of goals. Write the book. Once you have earned it, leverage it to advance your dreams and goals.

Professionally Design & Print Your roBot Book

When you are thinking about having your book professionally designed, remember that the inside of the book requires design just like the outside does. The idea is for the cover to be compelling enough that it interrupts the onlooker enough that they are curious enough to pick the book up. The title must be clear and the subtitle has to deliver a powerful promise so the person becomes more curious and flips the book over. The back of the book blurb should prompt the reader to want to know more, so they flip open the book to the table of contents. If the table of contents has a flow with sexy inviting titles, then you have compelled the reader to purchase the book. The first leg of your mission is complete. Now it is time for **The roBot Book Writing Method** to take over as they start reading. The Bot starts introducing the reader to your voice, your vision, and your value. Next, the Bot gets the reader interacting with you online while it is growing the know, like, and trust qualities unconsciously. The Bot gets the reader results and then he/she wants to connect with you, the author, to solve more of their problems.

While the reader is enjoying the content, it is equally important that the reader enjoys the experience of reading the book. Have your internal book designer break up the text with pictures, charts, scriptures, quotes, and other creative inputs. I like having the book done in color if color helps the reading experience. The book can be printed in black and white; however, you have the option to have a color print, even if it is at a later date. The internal design step should be done after the PROFESSIONAL BOOK EDITOR is 99% done with the project. The last one is allotted for looking at the completed project for printing.

One of the best things about self-publishing is you get to keep all of the profits. When I figured out I have the option of keeping all the profits, I was sold on the idea. The word, option, is important. You can sell the book from your funnel, sell in a store, sell online or at Amazon. You have full control over how much you are willing to accept as a profit.

Take Action

1. Using The roBot Book Method, choose a plan of action.
    a. Hire a team: Use a Done For You (DFY) method.
    b. Hire a Team: Use a Done With You (DWY) method.
    c. Utilize a How to Program or Done By You (DBY).
2. Choose an accountability partner and get their agreement to hold you accountable. If necessary, consider hiring a professional accountability partner.
3. Start the pre-sale process and start earning money prior to the books being shipped.

The Behavioral Reaction Automation

Dr. Tina Frizzell-Jenkins

Chapter 6

Blazing Trails of Trust

Blazing Trails of Trust

"Trust is built with consistency"
~ Lincoln Chafee

A good thing to keep top of mind in your business is that your business' reputation is everything. A definition of the word reputation is the beliefs or opinions that are generally held about someone. You want your business to be held in high esteem. **Phase Two of The roBot Book Writing Method is building the Behavioral Automation that plays a huge part in building authority, acquiring customers, and getting the highest value for your asset, your roBot Book.** Thinking about when you are shopping for a service or a product and the "stars" pop up. Almost unconsciously, most folks start to look for a four or five-star rating, especially if the vendor is unknown to them. This is the measuring stick of today. If you are the business owner, then you and your business are basically one and the same; therefore, being seen as a trustworthy individual is essential to the longevity of the business.

Building trust with your customers and clients has everything to do with keeping your word, doing what you say, and acknowledging when you or your business makes a mistake. Taking it a little further, **if a mistake is made, the goal should be to make the customer a little more than whole** as an act of goodwill. Statistics tell us that happy clients tend to be repeat clients. When someone purchases your roBot Book, they have answered the call of your voice and they will likely buy from you again as the roBot Book successfully does its job.

I recall, recently, I was doing a presentation on the Outline Your Next Book Challenge (a great opportunity for anyone to start their roBot Book) to jumpstart professionals and entrepreneurs on their authorship journey. A young lady who was in the General Admission was short-changed from watching the training live due to an error caused by my business. When I learned of the issue, I called her as soon as possible to apologize. She was very gracious about my phone call. Her disposition made it easy for me to upgrade her to VIP at no charge for the remainder of the challenge. That turned out to be a win for me and for the young lady. I put my best foot forward to right a wrong and she was able to get much more out of the challenge as she could ask questions and get solutions to her personal author journey. We parted with her being a happy customer. I expect we will work together again sometime in the future. Assess your trustworthiness below:

Self-Assessment: Trustworthiness Within Your Business Community

Below, rate yourself on a scale from 1-10 on how accurate the statements are – 1 means "not accurate at all" and 10 means "most accurate."

Once you've rated yourself for each statement, total up your scores and then use the Answer Key to determine your next steps. Take the Trustworthy Assessment below…

Trustworthiness Assessment	Self-Rating
In general, I am trusted in my business Community.	
I am able to accept credit for my products and services.	
I host live and virtual events.	
I am invited to participate in events with other influencers	
I pay my freelancers on time.	
I have 3 influencers inside my niche that will speak highly of me.	
I have 3 influencers outside my niche that will speak highly of me.	
I have collaborated on a project with 2-4 other business owners	
I have an affiliate program that pays out regularly.	
I have 5-10 customers that will give my product or service a four or five star rating	
Total Score	

Trust is essentially. It has to be earned; however, it is well worth it. Without being a trusted person in your business community and without the trust of your customers you can close the doors or your business because most folks are not buying the first time and repeat customers will likely be non-existent.

> Score 0-65
>
> Need to Build More Trust

The bad news is that you are not trustworthy in your business community likely because you may not have a business yet or you have not built up the authority necessary to have it, yet.

However, the good news is **The roBot Book Writing Method** can help. Creating **your roBot Book** will definitely jump start your authority as customers start to get the help your book provides from your product or service.

Reading this book and make notes on areas that you could use assistance. Get some [coaching](#) to expedite the process.

> Score 66-84
>
> You are Elevating Your Level of Trust

If your score landed you here, you are on track to write use **your roBot Book** and use it as a tool to draw customers to your backend (sales made as a result of the initial roBot Book purchase) product or service using **Behavioral Automation which is phase II for The roBot Book Writing Method**. Get some [coaching](#) to expedite the process.

> Score 85-100
>
> You are Trustworthy

Using **The roBot Book Writing Method** may literally cause a growth explosion in your business. As a Trustworthy business owner, you have position yourself to take full advantage of the **Behavioral and Business Growth Automations which are phase II and phase III of The roBot Book Writing Method**. Your calendar will likely stay booked. You will get to decide which customers you want to work with on your terms. If you would like some assistance with backend product or service options read Chapter 7 and Chapter 8 of **The roBot Book Writing Method** and if you need assistance contact us: https://launch-help.chatwithdrtinafj.com

Guarantee Your Trustworthiness

The best way to **guarantee your trustworthiness is to allow your action to speak louder than your words**, especially in adverse situations. Trust takes a long time to earn, and you can lose it quickly. Think of a time when you did not have much money and you were attempting to save. It took months or maybe years to grow your savings and then one major purchase, and the account all but evaporated. Think of a time perhaps when you were investing money and you wanted it to grow as fast as possible; therefore, you paid particular attention to what growth vehicle you planted it in, and you were diligent to seek other opportunities to grow your money. Trust is kind of like an investment. You want the best return on your behavior and you have to be willing to **seek opportunities to grow and foster goodwill**.

Genuinely Love the People You Serve

Loving the people, you serve should be easy if you are an authority figure in that community. However, it comes down to being in the correct community for you. Do you find yourself releasing negative energy regularly and repelling as you work with customers in your niche? If so, you may want to evaluate if you are in the right profession or business for you. Your negative energy is likely affecting your bottom line.

Remember from science class, energy is neither created nor destroyed. It just converts to another form. Therefore, any negative energy that you display with your customers can alter their attitude when working with you. You could very well be adding to the creation of a nasty undesirable customer. We have to check ourselves to make sure we are **exuding confidence and a delightful disposition** to attract the type of customer we desire to serve.

Get Results for the Customer

Customers are looking for results and your premium customers want an awesome experience, too. Your roBot Book is the first tool that introduces the customer to your world. The customer gets a feel for who you are and the results your business endeavors to provide when they read your book. We like to call the roBot Book the "Bot" which is short for roBot. The Bot starts to build the foundation of your customer acquisition process.

A roBot is a mechanical machine resembling a human being and able to replicate certain human functions automatically according to Wester. Since you cannot be everywhere, getting all your potential customers' results at the same time, your roBot Book is on assignment to get the masses having the desired result until you can make the personal connection with them. As a bonus, the type of customer who is willing to research and then purchase a book on a subject to learn something is likely a better customer than someone who is completely satisfied grabbing information or how-to from Google or an online resource that may or may not be credible.

Your roBot Book is your mouthpiece out in the world building belief in your products or services on your behalf. Convey all of your genius knowledge on a subject in your roBot Book and persuade the customer to take the action to get his or her desired result. When your customers feel like the roBot book **provides mega value**, they will naturally want to seek you out because your roBot Book got them results, for at least two reasons. The first reason is to see if other desired results can be obtained through other learning material you have or from you directly. The second is to get connected with like-minded individuals who can add value to their lives, individuals who are led by you, the authority figure.

By building trust, you, the expert, can help your customers to get over their biggest hurdles.

Let's Review ways to build trust with customers:

- if a mistake is made, the goal should be to make the customer a little more than whole
- guarantee your trustworthiness by allowing your action to speak louder than your words
- seek opportunities to grow and foster goodwill
- loving the people, you serve
- exuding confidence and a delightful disposition
- provide mega value

When you build trust, your customer AUTOMATION kicks in. They will **AUTOMATICALLY** tell others in their family, community, and even strangers about your products and services. This will boost the value of your roBot Book Asset!

Take Action

1. Request honest feedback from current customers to level up your "know, like & trust" attributes.
2. Find someone that has a problem in your community and help them.
3. Intentionally, do an act of goodwill for someone in your community, that has little or nothing to do with business.

Chapter 7

Build a Buzz for Your Business

Build a Buzz for Your Business

"The only way to advertise is by not focusing on the product"

~ Calvin Klein

Add a buzz around your business using **The roBot Book Writing Method**. Marketing buzz is the term used in viral marketing and is the interaction of customers and users of a product or service which amplifies the marketing message. As mentioned in the last chapter, **Phase Two of The roBot Book Writing Method is building the Behavioral Automation that plays a huge part in building authority, acquiring customers, and getting the highest value for you asset, your roBot Book. For this reason, you want the emotion, energy, excitement, and anticipation about a product or service to warrant a Buzz.**

That Buzz can be generated by international marketing activities by the brand owner or it can be the result of an independent event that enters public awareness through social or traditional media such as newspapers. Marketing buzz originally referred to oral communication but today's age of social media such as Facebook, Twitter, Instagram, and YouTube are now the dominant communication channels for marketing buzz. Some of the common tactics used to create buzz include building suspense around a launch, or event, creating curiosity, or reaching out to bloggers and social media influencers. Social media participants in any particular virtual community can be divided into three segments: influencers, individuals, and consumers. Influencers amplify both positive and negative messages to the target audiences, often because of their reputation within the community

Therefore, a successful social media campaign must find and engage with influencers who are positively inclined to the brand, providing them with product information and incentives to forward to the community. Individuals are members of the community who find value in absorbing the content and interacting with other members. The purpose of the marketing strategy is ultimately to turn individuals into the third group called customers, who actually purchase the product in the real world and then develop brand loyalty that forms the basis for ongoing positive marketing buzz. The challenge for the marketer is to understand the potential complex dynamics of the virtual community and be able to use them effectively.

Getting Brand Visible To Potential Customers

These Steps Can Help You Build The Buzz…

> **Go above and beyond.** According to research, 84% of consumers act based on personal recommendations. If your customers are excited, chances are they will tell others. So, make a practice of delivering outstanding products and services that set your business apart from the competition. Be Personable. Treat your clients with respect and patience. Listen to their concerns and go the extra mile to meet their needs.

Even small touches beyond the expected will demonstrate your goodwill and the commitment and care you will bring to your work.

Encourage Reviews. Online reviews are a huge opportunity to get exposure for your business. Today's consumers are researching online before making purchasing decisions, whether of a product or service, and 60% trust the opinions they read on the web, according to research. Yelp, Google – Plus, and other popular online directories are a form of free advertisement for your business and they reach a large audience.

Claim Your Listings. Create a business profile and ask your customers to share their experiences there. Also, encourage reviews on your website. Search engines love customer reviews and will reward your site with a higher ranking in search results. To increase the number of reviews for your business, don't be shy about asking your customers. If they are happy with their purchase or service, the customer will be inclined to follow through with a positive review. Provide a link on your business card or in an email. Customer feedback platforms such as Get Five Stars makes it easy for you to send an email invitation to your customers. They can respond with a rating and a paragraph or two about their experiences.

Think Out Of The Box. Experiment with unconventional ways to public curiosity and draw attention to your business. Make flashy flyers with catchy graphics and post them at locations where potential clients will see them. Run a contest on social media. Entice participants with the promise of a prize they care about and capture their email address for future marketing efforts. Offer free trials, discounts, and rebates. These are just a few ideas to help get you started. Gather your team together to brainstorm creative ideas to try for your business.

Be an In-Person Presence. It's easy to get caught up behind the computer with marketing by the way of email and social media, but an in-person presence is still the best way to make an impression. Get out and talk to people. Join networking groups and your local chamber of commerce, and go where prospects are inclined to be, such as conferences, meet-up groups, and industry events. Give a presentation or volunteer to serve on committees and within your community. Get involved in anything that will bring notice to your business and get people better acquainted with you. You will likely build new friendships and gain some new customers in the process.

Engage Online. The internet and social media offer a wealth of opportunities to engage with clients, understand what's important to them, and spread the word about your business.

Here Are Some Tips To Help Build Buzz Using Online Channels:

- Find and join online forums for your community and actively offer your expertise and response to consumer questions.
- Follow your customers on social media and encourage them to follow you. Respond in a calm way to all comments, questions, and especially complaints, and acknowledge with a thank you that shows you value your customers' business and point of view.
- Listen to what your customers are talking about online and respond with comments that address the top concerns. Write a post on Facebook or share an article on your website, honing in on topics that are top of mind and can quickly stimulate conversation and sharing.
- Being a guest blogger for an influential person who specializes in your line of work elevates your authority. Your reach will extend far beyond what they can achieve alone.
- Join in the conversation regularly as you find it appropriate. Your consistent presence will make you a familiar name and trusted expert among your readers.
- Keep the "buzz" alive. Build buzz so intensely that it will go viral and reach an ever-widening circle of people through the momentum of the conversation. Keep the word alive by continuously stoking the flames.

Deliver An Experience

Premium clients are looking for an experience when they make a purchase. Providing that experience goes a long way to creating a repeat client. Maybe you have noticed a number of videos that show the unboxing of cool electronics. The folks tend to get almost as excited with the unpacking as they are with the electronics. Ok, perhaps electronics is not your thing. How about travel? Have you taken a vacation at a fancy resort that is all-inclusive? They may have special staff support that picks you up and escorts you to your dinner location or you return to your room to find the covers turned down with chocolates and an animal display created out of flowers and towels. These kinds of extras change the vacation from just a vacation to a vacation experience that you can't stop talking about when you return home. This is the type of experience you want to provide for your customers in your business.

Consider sharing gifts with your clients through the mail, sharing meals with them at events, hosting events that go above and beyond, like hiring a comedian or a DJ. Think outside the box to determine what would bring significant value to your client's purchase. Make it a memory, so memorable that the client goes on and on about it long after the purchase is complete and tells others that they need to have the same experience. Remember the following three things when creating an experience for your clients:

- Education – a good book, value-added training, swag that stimulates conversations

- Edible Treats & Extravagant Meals – chocolate covered strawberries, wine, dinner for two at a high-end restaurant
- Entertainment – travel accommodations, day spa, two hours of horseback riding or golf.

Purpose to provide an experience for your customers and clients that speak volumes about your brand. In return, you will likely see many customers connecting with your business due to the best type of advertising, word of mouth.

Dope Customer Reviews

Having negative reviews about your business or your products and services will immediately turn customers away. **Having "dope" or good reviews is essential to your business thriving.** It is that simple. Customers do almost everything online and people use the internet to shop and conduct pre-purchase research. They compare brands, prices, and products, online. Nine out of ten customers use search engines like Google and Bing to do their online research before making a purchase. When researching, customers encounter online reviews – positive and negative on brands and products.

Loss Of Revenue – According to research, bad reviews on Google and Facebook have a significant effect on your revenue. A business with a 1 to 1.5-star rating reports 33% less revenue than the average enterprise. Research shows that 94% of customers avoid a company with bad reviews.

Undermine Business Reputation – negative reviews have the power to damage the reputation you have built for years. They make potential customers trust your business less. Many people do not purchase from a store with a bad reputation and questionable credibility. A large percentage of customers question the quality of a company with negative reviews. Abundant negative reviews are hard to fix and make it challenging to regain customers' trust.

Low Search Engine Ranking – Review ratings affect the way your business ranks on search engines. Negative rankings make your business rank poorly because search engines recommend the best enterprises to users.

How Good Reviews Affect Your Business – An online customer will often research customer reviews before making any online purchase. 90% of shoppers read at least one online review before going to a business storefront. Technology has increased the number of online customer reviews, as opposed to the past when a local business only had their in-person customer experience to consider. As a result, small local businesses need to manage their online reputation and monitor online customer reviews consistently. Online customer views can:

Increase Purchases – Social proof impacts sales decisions even if the majority of customer reviews are from strangers. A five-star rating on a product can be the deciding factor for an online customer to make a purchase they were not sure about. Customer feedback creates social proof that customer reviews increase buying and decrease the need for alternative marketing. Negative reviews also affect social proof by decreasing the likelihood of an online customer making a purchase.

Heighten Visibility – The higher your business rating is with the major search engines, the more likely a customer is to visit your site and potentially purchase your product or service. Aim to get your website, blogs, and social platforms ranking high on Google for example.

Foster Trust – Business reviews can ease the mind of an online customer who is unfamiliar with your business. We should show that an average customer review that is above a four-star rating will more likely result in a sale and increased site traffic. The more product reviews that your product receives, the more traffic your page will likely get. Make it easy for your customers to leave positive reviews. There is a small margin of error for the star rating that online customers will engage with.

Customers leave sites that have too many negative reviews and or low star ratings. Your company's reputation management should focus on getting positive reviews that foster trust online for your business. Remember an online customer may be hesitant to trust products that lack reviews altogether because of social proof.

Expand Reach – Encourage customers to leave online reviews and give customer feedback directly to your company on where you can improve. Positive views are more likely to be spread among online social media networks and businesses review sites like Yelp or Foursquare. Negative reviews can cause a lot of damage if they are not properly addressed with an effective reputation management program.

Raise Revenue – Positive online customer reviews lead to increased revenue. Just a one-star rating improvement on yelp can boost sales by 5 to 9% in the short term.

Create A Conversation – Online reviews are a great place for a local business to engage with its customers. Every negative review should be properly addressed and businesses should make all attempts to make up for customer experience issues. You should make sure to engage with positive reviews as well in order to show your local customers that you care about what customers say about you. Your customer service should always incorporate replying to online customer reviews.

Disseminate Vision Through Social Channels

Sharing content online allows you to craft an online presence that reflects your values and professional skills. Even if you only use social media occasionally, what you create, share, or react to, feeds into this public narrative. How you conduct yourself online is now just as important as your behavior offline, especially when it comes to your digital marketing career. Building your brand on social media takes more deliberate effort. Just think of what it takes to become instafamous! Your online image could help you land your next job opportunity or help you to foster valuable connections.

Fully update your social media accounts. Decide which social media accounts you are going to focus on and delete any old accounts that you no longer use. For the networks, you will be using, make sure all of your information is complete and accurate. This will help you to direct and grow traffic to the networks that will showcase yourself and your work. You should also remove any questionable content from the past that could have been seen as having a bad tone and does not have a positive effect on your personal image.

Identify your area of expertise. Everyone is an expert at something. When it comes to creating and distributing great content, we're having an Encyclopedic knowledge of your favorite TV show. Is it time for you to experiment a bit more? Think about what type of content you've created that your followers have responded to most. Can you replicate this with other similar content or repurpose something to reengage? The more unique and engaging content you create on your chosen topic of expertise, the more your followers will start to think of you as a leader in your chosen field. Regularly share content. In the early days of social media, the more you posted, the more engagement you could drum up. Today, however excessive posting leads to fatigue and annoyance. Do you want to keep the lines of communication open with your audience but you also don't want to over-share so much that you look desperate? The sweet spot is pulsing around 3 to 4 times a week for individuals.

Import your contacts, and you might be amazed to see how many people you already know on the social media networks you're using. There may be tens or even hundreds of people with whom you haven't yet connected. Import your email contacts from Google or Outlook, or contacts from your phonebook, into your social networks to find out how many connections you've been missing. Import from LinkedIn, Instagram, Facebook, and Twitter or allow for a free import of a certain number of contacts.

Keep Social Posts Positive and Engaging - It should be your goal to create an unstoppable online brand. Make sure the brand reflects you. Think of your interactions in content as a résumé of your work, and a reflection of your professional attitude and overall personality. Reposting other people's content can be valuable too.

Sharing content that you have written demonstrates your expertise. Find and join groups like Facebook and LinkedIn. They both offer thousands of opportunities to join groups focused on specific industries or topics. Just use the search bar on each network to find groups that are linked to your specific area of expertise. You will then be able to share insight and build authority around your brand. Keep in mind that industry groups may be overcrowded with competitors, so, smaller topic-based groups may be more fruitful in terms of reaching your audience.

Social Media Groups Can Help You:
- Challenge and motivate yourself
- Push you to achieve your goal
- Keep you accountable
- Generate ideas for your marketing
- Provide constructive feedback
- Build confidence
- Expand your skills
- Test your knowledge
- Develop leadership skills
- Contribute to others' missions
- Expand network & make friends
- Discover new opportunities.

Once you're a member of your preferred social media groups, don't be afraid to jump into discussions and add your unique insights. It can be challenging to remember that's exactly why social media works!

Keep your brand voice, image, and tone consistent. You probably already figured out that sticking to your defined personal image is important. If a particular political commentator suddenly and radically switches parties, no doubt they would lose a lot of fans overnight. You must also remain consistent with your ideas and the way you present them so that you're memorable and trustworthy. Finding the tone of your voice that works best for your brand may entail some trial and error, but there are personal branding guidelines you can use to determine the best fit for you. It's not as easy as saying, "I want to be funny," you need to further develop your ideas to support your approach.

Following your brand guidelines help to control people's perception. You can damage an otherwise flawless reputation if one of your profiles shows up with content or images that do not match your brand's voice. Build your brand by taking a social media and marketing course. The best way to build your brand on social media is to understand the fundamentals. Learn how to conduct social research to understand your audience, figure out content formats that will work for you. Create a strategy no matter how small, so you know where you want to go and how to get there. You also need to understand the ins and outs of each social media platform and what you can do to drive your unique message. With some practice, you'll soon learn what channels work best and how to measure success.

Buzz Marketing Summation:
Buzz marketing is a viral marketing technique focused on maximizing by word of mouth or media the potential of a product or service. The strategy can spur conversations among customers, family, and friends on social media platforms. Getting lots of consumers talking about your products or services creates the buzz

that grows awareness which in turn adds more and more online traffic that can increase sales and profits.

A brick and motor buzz marketing example could be a business intentionally showcasing their product in the parking lot of a superstore and letting customers try them out in real-time, and the event is happening in 50 states all on the same day. That would create a buzz.

An online buzz marketing example could be a business intentionally showcasing their product in the virtual parking lot where folks all across the country are going live showing customers try out a product in real-time, and the event is happening in 50 states and around the world all on the same day. That would create a buzz

Insert **The roBot Book Writing Method** into all of the aforementioned social platforms and processes to gain authority faster. Once the tool, in this case, your roBot book gets circulating your exposure multiplies. Once the exposure multiplies and the roBot Book does what it was designed to do the customers start to seek you out. Why? They get a solution to a problem they have, interact with the roBot book, complete self-assessments, and activities that clue them into where they are and how your business product or service might be what they require. When you build an awesome social reputation of providing good content AUTOMATION kicks in. Your fans will **AUTOMATICALLY** tell others in their family, community, and even to strangers about your products and services. This will boost your authority and the value of your roBot Book Asset!

Take Action

1. Decide which two social platforms best suit your lifestyle
2. Commit to a regular posting pattern
3. Schedule your posting time on a calendar.

BUSINESS GROWTH AUTOMATION

Dr. Tina Frizzell-Jenkins

Chapter 8

Big Bucks By Coaching

Big Bucks By Coaching

"Coaching transforms your thinking and alters your actions"

~ Dr. Tina Frizzell-Jenkins

Happy are clients whose coaching relationships get them the results they desire. Usually, the result that the client is looking for does not happen overnight. Coaching is a process that I like to say, transforms your thinking and alters your actions. Hang with me because I know not everyone is a coach or desires to be a coach. **Phase Three of The roBot Book Writing Method is Business Growth Automation and it plays a huge part in the next level of building authority, acquiring customers, and getting the highest value for your asset, your roBot Book.** Notice we are moving away from talking about customers to talking about clients. Clients are not just purchasing a product or service they are the individuals looking for and wanting to purchase professional services and advice.

You are the expert associated with your product or service and if you want to grow your business you have to level up your coaching and consulting skills to lead the folks that want to procure your services at a higher or premium level. These premium clients are willing to a pay premium cost to get the result they desire in a more intimate setting, at a faster pace, or done for them. The question is will you be ready? To assist in getting you ready Phase Three of **The**

roBot Book Writing Method must be activated. This method incorporates building some coaching skills especially if you are not a certified coach.

The coaching relationship is built on trust and mutual respect. The trust must be deep enough that the client can take the actions that are uncomfortable as the coach gives direction. Recognizing that the coach has been hired to facilitate a positive change. This is particularly necessary when speaking of business consulting/coaching.

Using **The roBot Book Writing Method** as your secret weapon to lead customers to your doorstep and eventually to becoming repeat paying clients is the real goal. At some point in the cycle of buying, you should desire to move the customer to become your client. As we discussed in the previous paragraph coaching can take time to be fully absorbed as well as utilized. Thus, the coaching relationship is necessary to formalize the time together to get the changes and results desired.

Coaching sessions are done one-to-one or in a group session. There are benefits to both methods of coaching. If the topic is highly personal or career-based, one-to-one coaching is likely best. If the coaching is business-related, group coaching ranks highest. Group coaching affords the opportunity for each member to learn from the questions and dialogue of the group. One person might ask a question that another member didn't think to ask or may not have ever asked. The coach gets to support several folks at once and eliminate answering the same questions multiple times. In addition, with many great minds in one room, innovation can be at its peak.

From a business perspective, group coaching is by far the best. Because when a Coach works with one client in an hour, they earn a fee, and when the Coach works with multiple clients during the same hour, they earn multiple fees. Group coaching is a time saver. The coach could have four one-on-one one-hour appointments or one appointment for an hour with four clients. Ultimately, you want to create the best coaching model that serves you and your business. Often, someone who has gotten results from your core value product or service is eager to become a coaching client to get more knowledge from you, the coach.

Create a Results-Driven Training

A results-driven training is designed to allow your client to have a measurable result at the completion of the training. The training can be a core value product offer service. For example, after participating in the Outline Your Next Book Challenge, participants will have the outline for their next book. After completing the training, participants are ready to put pen to paper to create their book to get their readers the results they know their readers desire to get using the outline as a guide.

The training generally takes place over five consecutive days for two hours a day or ten hours for the week. Those who participate at the VIP level have the opportunity to ask questions and get real-time coaching for their projects from the expert sharing valuable, useful, and usable information. The participant gets to have access to an expert who typically charges thousands of dollars an hour for the cost of an extremely reasonable training of say, $297.00. General admission participants register for approximately, $97.00. They get five hours of training; however, they do not receive any up-close interaction with the expert; thus, limiting their acceleration through the outline building process.

- Day 1 of the challenge evaluates the "Big Idea" of the book. The elements of the Big Idea are necessary to push the idea from an idea to a winning outcome. It is the well-thought-out strategy, the niche, and the ability to articulate with clarity so that almost anyone can understand.
- Day 2 of the challenge examines the book title and the sub-title. The Book title should be super clear and little to no guesswork required. The sub-title is a powerful promise that speaks to the results the reader can expect to have access to once the book is complete, and also small victories throughout the reading journey.
- Day 3: Participant learns to create an outline using outline-ology… the science structure of an outline. This is where the author connects with the reader by creating feelings, forecasting enough information to have the reader wanting more, and providing the fruit that produces the seed that grows into the outcome.
- Day 4, The Book Power day: Outlines have the power to push readers purposely through a rhythmic flow that helps

- to keep the reader focused on the content. Using the power of three points for easily remembering the content, picking the purpose of the discussion, and pitching the points necessary to move to conclusions.
- Day 5 hones in on the book's sales system or the Cash Machine, aka the Automatic Book TM. This is where Lead Generation Offers are born, Core Products Offers are put in place and Premium Value Offers seeding to produce fruit that seeds and produces more fruit.

You want to spend some quality time to create a course, a challenge, a Bootcamp, group coaching, an event, or some training product as a spin-off of your book. Creating a premium product is one of the fastest ways to grow your business and attaching a coaching program to it is next level. If you want help with growing your business contact us. https://launch-help.chatwithdrtinafj.com

Convey Your Message In Boot Camps

Once your tribe identifies with you and is ready to experience you in a more intimate learning environment, it is time to introduce them to a boot camp that you lead. The boot camp should be designed to assist the customer to grow through or with some well-thought-out sequences of movements that get them to their desired outcome as quickly as possible.

Around 2005, when I started hosting boot camps, I was busy creating content after content. I was hosting the boot camps via the Free Conference Call service, sometimes weekly. Although I was providing great value, I was not being the best leader. I was thinking that making everything about the learning experience as easy as I could, would be helping my tribe. No, I was creating a crutch and hindering their success. Leading/coaching is NOT about making it easy. **Leading/coaching is about creating a framework that is easy** that allows clients to grow on their journey with your support. Luckily, my heart was in the right place and a healthy number of those clients still show up and support my learning endeavors.

C. P. poet at heart
Speaking and writing are physically challenging
Open to learning about the options available to document her poetry
Determined not to let her situation steal her joy

Although C.P. is challenged with her "other abilities" with speaking, she was devoted to getting her poetry organized and available to be enjoyed. As a result of attending the Author Bootcamp, she was encouraged to start a writing group in her apartment complex. One of the best compliments a teacher can have is one of their students becoming the teacher and sharing what they have learned to continue the cycle of developing others.

Three Types of Boot Camps

The boot camps can be set up with three basic training features. They can be Grab It Training, Group Interaction Training, or Group Innovation Training.

Grab "it" training is a "done by you" learning experience. The client becomes a student and is signing on to a self-service training program. Perhaps there are a series of videos and/or audios with instructions explaining how to accomplish a "thing." There may also be some exercises or quiz material included to solidify that the student has a good grasp of the material presented.

Group Interaction Training is a "done with you" learning experience. The client, the coach, and the coach's team partner together to provide the customer with an elevated and faster results-driven learning experience. The client/student and the coach work together to get the results desired by the client. The result generally comes faster and there are opportunities to adjust, remove or add client particular inputs. Add the group coaching and the client's experience and personal growth are leveled up.

Group Innovation Training is the "done for you" experience that is more about getting the result as fast as possible with a level of understanding. It is not necessary that the client knows or learns all of the ins and outs of the process. The client is willing to pay a premium fee to save time and get the result into play and working on an accelerated timeline. The coach and the team capture the innovative knowledge of the client and insert it in their program or process and produce a result. A key role of the coach is to capture the genius of the client and put it on display within the constraints of the product or service provided.

Cultivate the Genius of Your Client

There is little more invigorating for me than to hear one of my students proclaim that my coaching helped them get their dream job, write a book, increase their income, move the level in the life of someone who has given them permission to speak into their life. Meaning what we learned on a journey together, they were able to share with someone else and make a difference. That's powerful stuff. What we have done together has elevated their genius. I believe that is the mission. I invite you to make it a mission for yourself with your clients.

Coach Like A Pro

Master these **5 Coaching Tools** to start your journey of Coaching like a professional coach.

<u>Active Listen Technique:</u>

Listening is the main staple or heart of coaching. You can provide so much value to your client just by listening and giving them the results, they desire. Listening really involves paying attention with all of your senses to hear and feel what is being said or not said by your client. Pay particular attention to their voice tone. The goal should be to use all sensory components and intuition to connect with the speaker's message.

Example of part of an Introduction business growth discussion...

Client: It was extremely challenging for me to get up an hour earlier and post on social media and send out engagement emails with my community.

Coach: It sounds like this is something you really want to do; however, you are so exhausted that you find it challenging and perhaps a little frustrating. What other time in the day might work better even though morning seems ideal?

Mirroring Technique:

The mirroring technique is about listening to what has been said and repeating it back to the client so the client feels like they have been heard and that you get what they are attempting to share with you.

Example of part of a Hurdle jumping discussion...

Client: Today started out as a normal day and I was basically on schedule with my events for the day. I received a phone call from my aunt that does my business book and she notice an accounting error that negatively affected my balance. My payment is going to be delayed 10 days. I am waiting for a major contract invoice to pay me. Can you give me a 10-day extension?

Coach: Good to hear from you, Charlie. I heard you say that your day was going well until you got an upsetting call from your accountant. An error caused a negative balance and you are expecting an invoice payment soon. You would like to delay your payment until you receive those funds. Did I get that correct?

Validating Technique:

Everyone has feelings and they have the right to have them. Your clients should not be made to feel guilty about their feelings. When you validate clients, you let them know that they have the right to their feeling. You have to stay in the non-judgment zone. Validating is not agreeing, not saying "the response" is right or wrong. Your intent should be to let the client know you can see their perspective. The objective is to get your client to release and feel "good with" having feelings about a particular thing.

When you validate never, never, never say you know how they feel because truly you don't even if you have been in a similar situation. You can say something like, you have the right to feel (be upset, uncomfortable, angry, distraught, etc.) the way you do because "the thing" was hurtful.

Example of part of a Sale closing discussion…

Client: I already paid a coach several thousand dollars and I did not get the results I wanted.

Coach: It's understandable that you are not pleased with spending money and not getting the results you desired. Would it be fair to say you learned what and what not to do in future transactions? .

Wait for a response.

Coach: respond to their response. You are equipped because the client just told you their issue.

Clarifying Technique:

This is a technique that you use not only for your understanding but to be sure the client has a clear understanding of the message they are attempting to get across. This is when you get the client to do the majority of the talking and you listen and ask the questions that provide you with answers that have definitions. If you miss what the client is saying you simply say these 5 great words, "tell me more about that."

Example of part of a Business Building discussion…

Client: I really want to build a business

Coach: What do you mean by build a business

Client: I guess what I mean is I want to earn extra income

Coach: Hmmm earning extra income is one thing; however, starting a business is another. How would you go about starting a business?

Getting Buy-in Technique:

Buy-in is all about "what's in it for them." The key is getting the client to be emotionally connected to something they really want that you can provide.

Example of part of a Joining Your Coaching Program discussion…

Client: I am struggling to incorporate exercise into my day. I always feel better when I exercise; yet, I don't do it.

Coach: I am guessing that when you exercise you not only feel better but you look better, your close fit better and you have more energy. Our Fitness coaching program is flexible and we pride ourselves on creating a time sensitive-program tailor-made for each client. How can we make this work for you?

Being able to effectively communicate with your clients using some of the basic tools of the trade will equip you to show up as the **expert on a higher level and gain the respect that causes AUTOMATION. Clients will AUTOMATICALLY share that having you as their coach is good for their business or good for getting the best use of a particular product or service.**

Self-Assessment: Coaching Skills

Below, rate yourself on a scale from 1-10 on how accurate the statements are – 1 means "not accurate at all" and 10 means "most accurate."

Once you've rated yourself for each statement, total up your scores and then use the Answer Key to determine your next steps.

Coaching Skills Assessment	Self-Rating
I thrive on cultivating the genius in others.	
I operate in a no-judgment zone.	
I have a coaching certification.	
I have proven coaching tools that I use with my clients.	
I am a good listener.	
I am a continuous learner.	
I have built credibility with the coaching skills	
I get excited to facilitate group coaching.	
I am competent in my mirroring skills.	
I operate ethically with coach-client confidentiality.	
Total Score	

Coaching is about making your way and putting your stamp/hand-print on the event, goal, innovation, etc. Consulting is about following another's path or way to get a similar result. In other words, when it comes to writing your book, coaching is helpful in making the outcome scream your name and consulting is about providing a framework to get your customers the end result they desire as quickly as possible.

What was your score?

Score 0-60
The Fundamentals of Coaching are Missing

The bad news is that your coaching qualities are missing core fundamentals. This is likely not a surprise to you.

However, the good news is that you can grow and improve on your core qualities. Get some coaching to expedite the process.

Reading this book will show you several areas where coaching will benefit your professional development and increasing the cashflow from your asset, the roBot book. Make mental notes on areas you desire to work on with a coach.

> Score 60-80
>
> Coach Skills are Leveling Up; therefore, Business can Level Up

If your score landed you here, you are on track to write your signature book that highlights your product or service. You should desire to get as much revenue as possible from the "back end" (profits generated after a book sale) profits. Get some coaching to expedite the process.

For you, the biggest hurdle to overcome is stomping out your limiting belief(s) about writing your book. Perhaps it is getting past, "no one will read my book, I am not a salesman, or you fill in the _____ blank. Review Chapter 5 for help with Limiting Beliefs.

Using **The roBot Book Writing Method** will assist you in crushing the limiting beliefs. The framework addresses how to get your book read, and how to get multiple streams of revenue without selling a single book or by selling multiple books at once. Knock the first domino down in the book writing process, join the challenge:

outlineyournextbookchallenge.com

> Score 80-100
> Coach Expert

Since your score landed you here, you are on track to write the book that is filled with the language necessary to build curiosity and encourage your customers to want to be their very best using your products or service.

For you, the biggest hurdle is likely carving out the time to get a quality book project done. One thing to remember, "done is better than perfect."

Using **The roBot Book Writing Method** will show how every year that goes by is more than time lost, but revenue loss too. When your intellectual property is being monetized and it can earn you an extra 5K-10K per month, that could equate to $60K - $120K dollars per year or more. Every year that passes from now going forward, you can be missing out on that $60K - $120K. Five years from now, on the low end, that could be $300K, and ten years from now, that could be $600,000.00. On the high side for this example, it could be $1.2M. You could buy a nice house, invest money for the future, and take the dream vacation.

If you would like some assistance with you're The roBot Book Writing Method contact us:

https://launch-help.chatwithdrtinafj.com

Remember, when you build up your coaching skill to provide top quality coaching to your clients you equip them to best utilize your products and services and you are positioning yourself to have premium clients and AUTOMATION kicks in. Now your premium clients will **AUTOMATICALLY** tell other premium clients about your products and services. This will boost the value of your roBot Book Asset and boost your authority! To take your business coaching to the next level, consider creating masterminds. Masterminds can play a big part in the next level of building authority, acquiring customers, and getting the highest value for your asset, your roBot Book

Utilize Coaching Skills with Masterminds

Masterminds are an experience and a game-changer. Masterminds become an extension of your interpersonal communication where you and at least two more individuals are involved in an exchange of ideas, skills, and interests. Together with a common goal, you interact with one another to accomplish that goal, recognize one another's existence and see yourselves as part of the group using the Mastermind as the platform. The means of interaction depends on different factors like availability, cost implications, and technology preferences. The idea is based on the old saying that two heads are better than one. Therefore, working alone can cause an unbiased execution of ideas that can be limited in potential, and no one wants that who wants to grow and flourish.

The knowledge gained in masterminds can drastically grow your business as you learn from the genius of other business owners. Want to join a Mastermind? Search your topic online or get a referral from an influencer in the community. If you can't one be bold and start one yourself. Masterminds work well in a number of businesses like the following Money-Making Opportunities:

Online [Topic] Business

Making money online is the sweet spot people look for in the gig economy. Whether you aspire to be a six-figure social media influencer or are just looking to supplement your regular income with an internet business.

Affiliate Market

Affiliate marketing is one of the oldest online moneymakers available online. Here's how it works: As an internet entrepreneur, you'll need your web presence: website, blog, social media platforms, landing pages, sales pages, banner ads, or e-commerce site. But instead of selling your products, you sell the products of other companies. When customers on your digital platform click on a link to make a purchase, they are taken to your affiliate partner's site to complete the transaction and you get a commission for every completed sale. The best part is you don't have to deal with shipping or customer service. Affiliate marketing is one of the fastest and easiest ways to start an online business because all you have to do is promote the products. You don't have to worry about creating products, setting up payment and delivery systems, or handling customer support. You just simply drive the traffic and get them to click over to the companies you are promoting as an affiliate and if a sale is made, you get a commission for referring that sale.

Selling On Amazon, eBay, Etsy, And Craigslist

One of the quickest ways to get started selling online is to leverage the power of third-party sites. E-commerce giants like Amazon, eBay, Etsy, and Craigslist are powerful sales and marketing platforms with a built-in prospect base. Millions of people regularly shop on these sites, and the numbers keep growing. These mega-sites make it easy to set up so customers can browse your products, and there's no need to build your website. Also, you'll find a built-in search feature so that interested buyers can easily find your online storefront. Plus, you get to use the site's shopping cart. In short, you avoid a lot of the expense and hassle of setting up an independent e-commerce website.

Self-Assessment: Leadership

Below, rate yourself on a scale from 1-5 on how accurate the statements are – 1 means "not accurate at all" and 5 means "most accurate."

Once you've rated yourself for each statement, total up your scores and then use the Answer Key to determine your next steps.

Leadership Assessment	Self-Rating
I Genuinely like mentoring others to build their skillset.	

I am a continuous learner.	
I am innovative.	
I consider myself a visionary.	
I can be very flexible.	
I inspire others.	
I am dependable when challenges arise.	
I am non-judgmental.	
I encourage strategic thinking.	
I consider myself open-minded.	
My followers consider me open-minded.	
I have good delegation skills.	
In the eyes of others, I am trustworthy.	
I am passionate about the growth of others.	
I am a good communicator.	
I have good decision-making capabilities.	
I am accountable to my customers.	
I reflect intentionally on issues.	
I have top motivating skills.	
I have tolerance for mistakes.	
Total Score	

Leaders are readers. Leaders attract followers who look to them for vision, advice, and growth, to name a few. Most leaders have the ability to become an author quickly by sharing their knowledge and ability to teach a mindset and a skillset to folks who give them permission to speak into their lives. Leaders can generally provide lots of stories and case studies in their book to help the book carry more intellectual and hands-on weight.

> Score 0-60
> The Fundamentals of Leadership are Missing

The bad news is that your leadership qualities are missing core fundamentals. This is likely not a surprise to you.

However, the good news is that you can grow and improve on your core qualities. Get some coaching to expedite the process.

Read this book with an open mind and make notes of 1 or 2 areas that you can excel in and study to master. You may have to review the chapters you have already completed. Next, intentionally mentor someone else to be great along with you.

> Score 61-75
> Leader at Heart and Growing

If your score landed you here, you are on track to write the book that will assist you in attracting better customers. Better customers will give you better sales conversion rates.

Find a good hook for your short book, coupled with the Big Idea with Air and you will be on the right road. You'll be on the road to meeting your goals building authority, acquiring customers, and adding new revenue streams.

Currently, you are likely relying on marketing strategies that are not working the best for you. No worries, **The roBot Book Writing**

Method is just the framework you need to have a steady flow of the right customers.

> Score 76-100
>
> Leadership Expert

Since your score landed you here, it is safe to say that you are the type of expert who followers love to follow. This should excite you!

For you, the biggest hurdle to overcome is what tools you need to use to get your book done. Will you write it yourself using the computer or the hands-free method of using a scribe application? Perhaps, you can answer a series of questions so a ghostwriter can do the writing for you. You get to make the choice. Using **The roBot Book Writing Method** will afford you the opportunity to maximize your reach with your message and cause customers to seek you out. This will naturally increase your cash flow when using the Book TM™ to generate big bucks while attracting clients to lock arms with you and learn from you in one of your coaching programs or premium courses. Knock the first domino down in the book writing process, join the challenge: outlineyournextbookchallenge.com

Or if you would like some assistance in working through The roBot Book Method: https://launch-help.chatwithdrtinafj.com

Take Action

1. Practice two coaching skills on an associate and get feedback.
2. Join a group discussion in your niche. Listen for an issue that someone else is having. Take notes on the feedback given by the expert. Determine how the feedback may help you now or in the future.
3. What type of roBot Book product extension appeals to you and would work well with your business (i.e., a course, a challenge, etc.). Set a date within the next two weeks to have a short product description written out to share with a trusted associate.

Chapter 9

Benefits for Your Business with Your Self Care

Benefits for Your Business with Your Self Care

"People rarely succeed unless they have fun in what they are doing" ~ Dale Carnegie

If you want to have a successful business the process starts with you. Therefore, your self-care is an essential component in the growth, and the long-term existence of your business. Self-care is a factor in our mental, physical, emotional, social, spiritual, and intellectual being. One might suggest that some factors are more important in your business than others. Since we are all different it seems logical to me that the type of self-care I need may vary from what you need. That said, let's take a closer look at a few that may spark creativity in your business. Physical self-care has a lot to do with your body, so eating right and drinking your water. Emotional self-care in your business can be tied to your mastery and confidence in regards to your product or service. Lastly, your mental state should be clear so your creativity can flow. Let's examine these three a bit closer starting with…

Maximize Your Energy with Health Hack

As a business owner you can get extremely busy when launching a new product or service or with getting the business to the next level. However, you need to keep your energy up and practice good health habits. Below are a few health hacks to help:

- Blue Light Glasses can be stylish as well as protective. They protect your eyes from harmful blue light from computer and phone screens.

- Healthy Food in a Box can be a time saver and healthier. Consider getting a subscription to start preparing healthy meals a few times a week at home.

- Drink water and stay hydrated. Drink more water and limit the sugared drinks Also, drink lemon water first thing in the morning. Lemons have all sorts of wonderful vitamins, nutrients and antioxidants that can boost energy, reduce inflammation, improve your immune system, clear up your skin, and aid in digestion.

- Get more sleep. Invest in a mattress that helps you sleep better.

- Bodyweight exercises are great when there is no gym. Practice with pull-ups. Place a Pull Up Bar in the doorway. Start pulling yourself up repeatedly. Your body is now the weight.

- Cold showers improve circulation, increase metabolism, tighten pores, boost immunity and alertness.

- Try Laughter Yoga. Laughter will boost your immune system, lowering stress, reducing pain and preventing heart disease. Laughter is considered by many health professionals to be one of nature's best medicines for both mental and physical health.

Mastery Builds the Confidence

Confidence is a key contributor to mastery. That said, how can you build your confidence? Confidence makes you a more effective communicator, a stronger leader, and a more proactive and productive entrepreneur while building your business. Establishing new habits takes practice so to improve your confidence pick one of the techniques below in your business growth journey until you are comfortable with your results, and then tackle another one.

Below are a few tips:

Manage Your Confidence

Confidence is often reflected in how we show up. The two traits people will most often notice are your posture and gaze. To optimize your posture, roll your shoulders back to straighten your back, and try widening your stance slightly. To optimize your gaze, try a 2-millimeter shift. Lift your eyes and your head by 2 millimeters. Usually, look straight ahead or even slightly downward depending on how confident you're feeling. This slight shift instantly gives you a sense of confidence. Body language not only affects how people see you, it also affects how you feel.

Manage Your Confidence with Your Product or Service

Done is better than perfect. Get your product or service in the market. Don't hold it back until it's perfect. As soon as you launch, you'll get feedback from your customers and the market, you'll make your product or service better, and in the end, you'll save a ton of time and energy, and money by avoiding rework. Software developers, especially, tend to over-design and overdevelop before launching. This is problematic if you're not certain yet of whether the overall product meets your customers' needs.

To avoid a failed course, build a minimum viable product (MVP) and launch with what you can. An MVP is not supposed to be a product that you're proud of. It just needs to have the critical features that will allow you to find out if your product or service is something the market is willing to pay for and that you can feasibly produce. Once you get market feedback, keep building your business while you're flying it.

Practice Confidence

Don't wait to feel confident. Instead, take daily actions to stretch your confidence "muscles." Just like an athlete, you can't expect to be good at something unless you practice it every day. Ask yourself daily, "How can I practice confidence right now?" Perhaps you'll feel inspired to follow up on a prospect, ask your boss for a meeting to discuss your career, follow up on an email you're avoiding, or take 5 minutes to work on a problem you don't yet have any idea how to solve. You will be building the confidence muscle.

Meditate To Activate Innovation

It is a fact that many influencers meditate. They may or may not use the traditional meditation practices; however, it is in the quiet think time that innovation happens. **The roBot Book Writing Method** includes meditation as a way of intentionally tapping into your creative juices to grow your business. The right innovation will eventually become an AUTOMATIC system that produces results much like your roBot Book. Your think time is the most important time you spend in your business.

Meditation can also support your happiness and can improve your mood. It shifts your perspective. With less stress, and calmer, focused attention, you're allowed more of a bird's eye perspective (the elevated view of an object from above instead of staying down in the weeds and remaining confused). Getting good at Meditation takes time, yes, but it also saves time down the road. Meditation can improve your business in the following ways:

Mindset Growth Development

Avoid focusing on who you are instead of focusing on what you can change and improve. A growth mindset will help you take constructive feedback and work on yourself without lowering your self-confidence. It's also important not to take failure personally. It can be easy for entrepreneurs to attach a high level of their self-worth to their work performance. Always remember that you are much more than what you do at work.

Lessen the Stress

The most popular benefit of meditation is that it helps trim down stress. Everyday business interactions induce anxiety and can be burdensome. When we meditate, the effects start to show in our interactions with various people in the workplace. This helps reduce the chaos and anger which are a result of disagreement.

Maximize Performance

Meditation that is practiced behind closed doors can have a direct impact on the revenue that the business generates. Meditation is known to help maximize your performance.

useful ideas. If you are looking for some creative inspiration, whether it's to solve a problem or generate new and useful ideas, you can take a walk outside or collaborate with your colleagues. But have you tried meditation?

Meditation Tips for Creativity

Take The Time: While it's true that the creative spark can arrive at any time, creativity isn't a wild animal you have to coax out of hiding. Focus and attention are as beneficial to creativity as anything else. Giving yourself time to focus on being creative will do wonders for your output.

Meditate With A Goal In Mind: Whether you're writing a novel or creatively approaching a business problem, try meditating on the problem. Begin your practice as usual. Then summon the problem or character or plot point and give it your full attention. Incorporate it into your practice, along with your breath, and allow it to unwind and transform in your mind. You'll be surprised where your mind takes you when you focus on a single topic.

Stop, Collaborate, And Listen: If you reach a stalemate with an idea and have exhausted all possible avenues, take the idea out of your head and share it with others. If meditation gives you another perspective, two or three other minds will provide even further perspectives. You don't have to take anyone's advice, but their thoughts may take you in exciting new directions.

Open Up: At its core, creativity is about being open to possibility. Mindfulness meditation allows us to observe more possibilities than staring at a blank page our blinking cursor will allow. While meditating on a problem, indulge in some blue-sky thinking. (Blue-sky thinking is the activity of trying to find completely new ideas, "out of the blue sky.") Don't limit yourself to what's practical, let the possibilities soar.

Stress Less: It's very easy not to start, especially when we convince ourselves that whatever we start will go wrong or not work out. Meditation helps to ground our thinking and strip away the negativity that can kill creativity. .

Meditation Microdose: Similar to taking a nap, small doses of meditation can be refreshing. It's important to give your brain intermittent downtime to move into free-form thought or to just change gears from a continuous task. Next time you're sitting down to a project, set a timer for a short 3 to 5 minutes meditation break. You'll come back to work refreshed and potentially have the ability to prime more creative thought.

With meditation, you can make better decisions for yourself and your business. You can also respond more appropriately to anything that comes up, good or bad. You can be less impulsive or reactionary because when you're better balanced with your thoughts, with an improved mood, and better focus you will make better decisions. Also, when you're working from a less stressed or anxious palace, you'll make better decisions. Meditation is a tool that can allow you to have a better big-picture understanding of the situations; thus leveling you up as a better leader and business owner.

When you show up and shine in a Mastermind group with confidence and your expertise is on display you will gain the respect of others in the group. When Mastermind members are approached by someone looking for a service or product you offer they will remember you because you have served the group well. Thus, the AUTOMATION kicks in, and you are **AUTOMATICALLY** introduced by a fellow Mastermind participant to another possible premium client. This boosts your authority!

Self-Assessment: Creativity

Below, rate yourself on a scale from 1-10 on how accurate the statements are – 1 means "not accurate at all" and 10 means "most accurate."

Once you've rated yourself for each statement, total up your scores and then use the Answer Key to determine your next steps.

Creativity Assessment	Self-Rating
I can get very enthusiastic about things that excite me.	
I am innovative.	
I do not enjoy unpredictable outcomes.	
I feel that a logic base & step by step method works best when solving a problem.	
I am more interested in old ideas than new ideas.	
I am self-motivating.	
I find myself in search of inspiration regularly.	
I get great ideas when I pause and I am at peace.	
I like overlooking the rule, business before pleasure.	
I think perfection is overrated.	

Total Score	

The Creative thinking process can be mysterious to some, and invigorating to others. Nonetheless, different stimuli can activate your creative juices and **automatically you create a work of art, your roBot Book.**

| Score 0-60 |
| Creativity Is Not One of Your Top Strength |

The bad news is that your creative qualities are not your strong traits. This is likely not a surprise to you.

However, the good news is that you can seek help to advance any project you wish to accomplish. There are exceptional creative freelancers who make a living bringing the creative spark to your projects. Get some <u>coaching</u> to expedite the process.

This book has some definite steps you can take to bridge the creative gap quickly while sharing your expertise with your writing. Consider leaving the creativity to **The roBot Book Writing Method** Team.

| Score 61-75 |
| Creativity Is On the Rise! |

If your score landed you here, you have some creative bones in your body, so to speak.

Creative folks tend not to have very dominant answers to questions, you tend to think of more uses for a common object, and you tend to believe that creativity is fundamental to human life. You make great authors. You deliver your expertise so the masses have the opportunity to gleam from it.

Combine your creativity with **The roBot Book Writing Method** and your book project has the ingredients for success. Get started creating your roBot Book asset, today

> Score 76-100
> You Are Creative!

Since your score landed you here, it is safe to say that you are the creative type.

For you, the biggest hurdle to overcome is likely a shift in mindset. Sarnoff Mednick argued that people can achieve a creative solution through serendipity, similarity and mediation

Using **The roBot Book Writing Method** will equip you with the knowledge and tools to complete your book project. Knock the first domino down in the book writing process, join the challenge: outlineyournextbookchallenge.com

Or if you would like some assistance in working through The roBot Book Method: https://launch-help.chatwithdrtinafj.com

Take Action Now...

1. Identify a health hack and commit to making "it" work for you over the next month.
2. Choose a new skill to master and journal how the mastery is improving business over the next six months.
3. Start meditating for 10-15 minutes 2-4 times a week. Set a specific goal to intentionally spark creativity... Like writing your book with **The roBot Book Writing Method.**

Dr. Tina Frizzell-Jenkins

Chapter 10

Best Business Marketing Decision

Best Business Marketing Decision ...

> *"Wherever you see a successful business, someone once made a courageous decision.* ~ Peter Drucker

The best business marketing decision is using a book with robotic qualities to build belief in your brand on your behalf. **The roBot Book Writing Method** is the framework designed to assist professionals and entrepreneurs to create that reality for their business.

LET'S REVIEW...

The roBot Book Writing Method will replicate the benefits of your business automatically through the pages of your book. This is done by adding interactive content to heighten the awareness of your brand. Interactive activities include links to assessments, surveys, posts, testimonials, templates, and personal Q&A services, to name a few. Every time the machine (roBot Book) resembles a human being (asking questions like an assessment) and is able to replicate certain human movements (getting someone to take actions via the activity at the end of each chapter and share with another real human) and functions (video interactions) **automatically the roBot Book tool is working!**

What To Do Next....

Take your Big Idea and start writing your outline. Get the support that will best serve you in getting the book from the Big Idea to Building Belief in your Brand to Best Seller, if you desire that support.

How To Get Help?

Join The roBot Book Writing Method Team

Join the challenge ... outlineyournextbookchallenge.com

How to get help... connect@robotthebookmethod.com

Dr. Tina Frizzell-Jenkins

About The Author

Dr. Tina Frizzell-Jenkins, aka Coach Tina FJ, is an ICF certified executive and business coach, and founder of JTI, LLC.

She takes **AIM** with her clients to increase their **A**uthority, **I**nfluence, and **M**arketing so they can do what they love, do it better, and faster while multiplying their message, impact, and income. Her philosophy encourages the position of resisting the ordinary to do the extraordinary.

Coach Tina is a retired NASA engineer, where she also managed the NASA, Goddard's coaching bench staffed with internal and external coaches for six years, after her 25 years as an engineer. Tina has worked CEOs, executives to everyday individuals who want to develop personally. She and her clients have tackled interpersonal effectiveness, tactical & effective leadership, effectively communicating, organizational change, work-life balance, strategic career moves, launching entrepreneur endeavors, and getting results with teams.

Coach Tina FJ is the author of 6 books. Book number 3 is "Coaching Conversations." Struggling all her life to conquer the challenges of dyslexia, Coach Tina knows how to implement systems to beat obstacles and press on to success. Thus, she has been the book writing coach for multiple individuals writing their first non-fiction book without any previous book writing experience. She has also assisted first-time book writers in embracing and flourishing as entrepreneurs. Lastly, Coach Tina is the creator of **The roBot Book Writing Method.**

Coach Tina is a Professional Certified Coach, credentialed with the International Coaching Federation (ICF), and a proud graduate of the Institute for Professional Excellence in Coaching (iPEC).

Coach Tina is a native Washingtonian; however, she makes her home in Maryland with her high school sweetheart/husband, Willis. They have two adult daughters and a Yorkie. The entire family enjoys Maryland crabs and homemade chocolate chip cookies.

RESOURCES

CONTACT AND CONNECT

JUST TRADERS INTERNATIONAL, LLC

connect@coachtinafj.com

240-718-8462

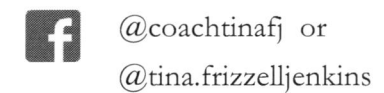

@coachtinafj

@coachtinafj or
@tina.frizzelljenkins

@coachtinafj

Other Literary Works

by the Author

Web Address

coachtinafj.com

Email

connect@tinafrizzell.com

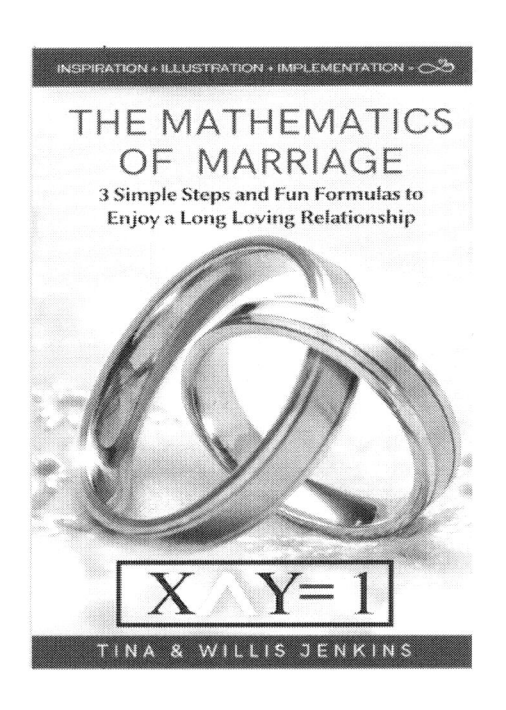

Web Address

mathofmarriage.com

Email

connect@tinafrizzell.com

What If You Could Get Your Book to Write Itself?

AiM CHALLENGE
Outline Your Next Book

Spend 5 Days with Me During This Challenge and I'll Show You How an Outline Puts Your Book Writing on Autopilot, Creates an Asset, and 5X-10X Your Customer Acquisition.

outlineyournextbookchallenge.com

Made in the USA
Columbia, SC
26 December 2022